W9-BGZ-236

Workbook to Accompany *The Structure of English*

Workbook to Accompany
The Structure
of English

Jeanette S. DeCarrico

Carol S. Franks

Portland State University

Ann Arbor

THE UNIVERSITY OF MICHIGAN PRESS

Copyright © by the University of Michigan 2000
All rights reserved
ISBN 0-472-08631-6
Published in the United States of America by
The University of Michigan Press
Manufactured in the United States of America

2011   2010   2009   2008   6   5   4   3

No part of this publication may be reproduced,
stored in a retrieval system, or transmitted in any
form or by any means, electronic, mechanical, or
otherwise, without the written permission of the
publisher.

ISBN 978-0-472-08631-3

Preface

The exercises in this book have been designed to accompany *The Structure of English: Studies in Form and Function for Language Teaching,* by Jeanette S. DeCarrico. Practice exercises are included for all major points covered in each chapter. A unique feature of this workbook is that, as in the textbook itself, passages from novels, short stories, drama, poems, and essays have been carefully chosen to provide a rich context that highlights the grammatical points under discussion. Because these excerpts are from the works of some of our most prominent writers, they also showcase *use* of grammar in contexts that illustrate how particular discourse functions of grammar contribute in important ways to more effective expression.

The exercises fall into several groups. Following the general format of the textbook, the exercises are grouped for practice that focuses on *form,* on *grammatical function* (i.e., sentence level function), and on *discourse function* of the grammatical categories. The less difficult ones emphasizing form are, with few exceptions, grouped in the beginning of each chapter, and they typically provide practice in identifying and using grammatical elements. These are followed by a second type, a bit more advanced, asking students to recognize the grammatical functions of these forms within the sentence. The third, most advanced exercises are those requiring students to think about particular discourse functions of grammatical categories and asking them to discuss or comment on these functions.

In later chapters especially, exercises are designed to draw more attention to these sentence and discourse functions in terms of improving the overall coherence of the discourse. In all cases, the exercises are closely tied to key parts of the discussion in the text. The ultimate goal of the practice is to complement the discussion in the text, which progresses in each chapter from an emphasis on knowledge of forms and functions of grammar to increased competence in using grammar for effective speaking and writing.

The versatile format of the exercises also allows for variety in the type of assignment given. Any or all may be assigned as graded or ungraded homework. For those providing practice with form or grammatical function, the answer forms are designed so that they can be easily checked against an answer key, available separately. The more advanced exercises asking for comment or discussion can also be assigned as either graded or ungraded homework. Alternatively, any of the exercises could be used for in-class practice sessions or small group discussions, or they could be used as questions for quizzes or other exams.

Acknowledgments

Our thanks to Suzanne Jacobs for comments on a preliminary version of the manuscript and to Elaine Limbaugh, Lorraine Mercer, Shelley Reece, and Karen Zagona for helpful suggestions concerning illustrative material. Thanks also to Patricia Joy Hyatt and Carol Fokine for help in proofreading the final version of the manuscript.

In addition, the following people and organizations are gratefully acknowledged for allowing their works to be included in this text.

Henry Holt and Company, Inc., for "A Considerable Speck" by Robert Frost, from *The Poetry of Robert Frost,* edited by Edward Connery Lathem. Copyright 1936, 1942 by Robert Frost, © 1964, 1970 by Lesley Frost Ballantine, © 1969 by Henry Holt and Company. Reprinted by permission of Henry Holt and Company.

Liveright Publishing Corporation for "Spring is like a perhaps hand," copyright 1923, 1925, 1951, 1953, © 1991 by the Trustees for the E. E. Cummings Trust. Copyright © 1976 by George James Firmage, from *Complete Poems: 1904–1962* by E. E. Cummings. Edited by George J. Firmage. Reprinted by permission of Liveright Publishing Corporation.

New Directions Publishing Corporation for "The Red Wheelbarrow," by William Carlos Williams, from *Collected Poems: 1909–1939, Volume 1.* Copyright © 1938 by New Directions Publishing Corp. Reprinted by permission of New Directions Publishing Corp. and Carcanet Press Limited.

Penguin USA for "When I Read Shakespeare" by D. H. Lawrence, from *The Complete Poems of D. H. Lawrence* by D. H. Lawrence, edited by V. de Sola Pinto and F. W. Roberts. Copyright © 1964, 1971 by Angelo Ravagli and C. M. Weekley, Executors of the Estate of Frieda Lawrence Ravagli. Used by permission of Viking Penguin, a division of Penguin Putnam Inc., and Lawrence Pollinger Limited.

A. P. Watts Ltd. for "The Wild Swans at Coole" by William Butler Yeats. Reprinted by permission of A. P. Watts Ltd. on behalf of Michael B. Yeats.

The Wylie Agency for "Goodbye, My Brother" by John Cheever. Copyright © 1951 by John Cheever, as printed in *The New Yorker.*

Every effort has been made to trace the ownership of all copyrighted material in this book and to obtain permission for its use.

Contents

Chapter 4. The Basic Verb Phrase

Chapter 5. Verb Classes and Sentence Types

Chapter 6. Pronouns, Pro-forms, and Ellipsis

Chapter 7. Prepositions and Prepositional Phrases

Chapter 1

A Brief Overview of the English Sentence

Exercise 1. Parts of Speech

For each underlined word in the following passage, from Toni Morrison's novel *The Bluest Eye,* indicate the part of speech by writing it in the corresponding blank following the passage. Use the abbreviations in the list. (*Note:* Not all parts of speech appear in the passage.)

N (Noun)	ART (Article)
ADJ (Adjective)	PRO (Pronoun)
ADV (Adverb)	PREP (Preposition)
V (Verb)	CONJ (Conjunction)

My daddy's (1) <u>face</u> is a study. (2) <u>Winter</u> moves (3) <u>into</u> it (4) <u>and</u> (5) <u>presides</u> there. His eyes (6) <u>become</u> a (7) <u>cliff</u> of snow threatening to avalanche; his eyebrows bend like (8) <u>black</u> limbs of (9) <u>leafless</u> trees. His skin takes on the pale, cheerless yellow winter sun; for a jaw he (10) <u>has</u> the edges of (11) <u>a</u> snowbound field dotted (12) <u>with</u> stubble; his (13) <u>high</u> forehead (14) <u>is</u> the frozen sweep of the Erie, hiding currents of gelid thoughts that eddy in darkness. Wolf killer turned hawk fighter, (15) <u>he</u> worked night and day to keep one from the door and (16) <u>the</u> other from under the windowsills. A Vulcan guarding the flames, he gives (17) <u>us</u> instructions about which doors to keep closed (18) <u>or</u> opened for (19) <u>proper</u> distribution of heat, lays kindling by, discusses qualities of coal, and teaches us how to rake, feed, and bank the fire. And he will not (20) <u>unrazor</u> his lips until spring.

1. _N_   5. _V_
2. _N_   6. _V_
3. _Prep._   7. _N_
4. _conj._   8. _ADJ_

1

9. ADJ

15. PRO

10. V

16. ART

11. ART

17. PRO

12. prep

18. CONJ

13. ADJ

19. ADJ

14. V

20. V

Exercise 2. Parts of Speech: Open and Closed Classes

Identify the underlined words in this passage, from Mark Twain's *Pudd'nhead Wilson,* by writing the corresponding abbreviations in the first column following the passage. Use the abbreviations in the list. Then decide whether each word belongs to the open or closed class and write accordingly either O or C in the second column.

N   (Noun)   ART   (Article)
ADJ (Adjective)   PRO   (Pronoun)
ADV (Adverb)   PREP   (Preposition)
V   (Verb)   CONJ   (Conjunction)

There is no (1) <u>character</u>, howsoever good and (2) <u>fine</u>, but it can be (3) <u>destroyed</u> by (4) <u>ridicule</u>, howsoever poor (5) <u>and</u> witless. Observe the (6) <u>ass</u>, for instance: his character is about perfect, he is the choicest (7) <u>spirit</u> among all (8) <u>the</u> humbler animals, yet see what ridicule has (9) <u>brought</u> him to. Instead (10) <u>of</u> feeling complimented when we are called an ass, we are left in doubt.

Part of Speech   *Open or Closed Class*

1. _____   ___

2. _____   ___

3. _____   ___

4. _____   ___

5. _____   ___

6. _____   ___

7. _____   ___

8. _____   —

9. _____   —

10. _____   —

Exercise 3. Identifying Units within the Predicate

In this exercise, (i) underline all occurrences of main verbs and auxiliaries and (ii) write either MAIN V or AUX above the ones you underline. Consider only the structures enclosed in brackets. The passage is again from Mark Twain's *Pudd'nhead Wilson,* repeated from exercise 2.

(1) [There is no character], howsoever good and fine, but (2) [it can be destroyed] by ridicule, howsoever poor and witless. (3) [Observe the ass], for instance: (4) [his character is about perfect], he is the choicest spirit among all the humbler animals, yet see (5) [what ridicule has brought him to]. Instead of feeling complimented (6) [when we are called an ass], we are left in doubt.

Exercise 4. Subjects and Predicates

Locate the subjects and predicates in these poems. Underline the subjects once; underline the predicates twice. (*Hint:* (1) First locate the verb; then turn the sentence into a *yes-no* question. The subject is the part that changes places with the first element of the verb. (2) Next, locate the predicate as the verb unit plus whatever follows it—including adverbials.) Follow the example.

Example: Some say the world will end in fire.

SUBJ   PRED
Do some   say the world will end in fire?

Thus: Some say the world will end in fire.

THE RED WHEELBARROW
William Carlos Williams

So much depends

upon

a red wheel
barrow

glazed with rain
water

beside the white
chickens.

NOTHING GOLD CAN STAY
Robert Frost

Nature's first green is gold,
Her hardest hue to hold.
Her early leaf's a flower;
But only so an hour.
Then leaf subsides to leaf.
So Eden sank to grief,
So dawn goes down to day.
Nothing gold can stay.

Exercise 5. Recognizing Verb Types

In this passage, from Deirdre McNamer's novel *Rima in the Weeds,* identify the underlined verbs according to type by writing the corresponding numbers in the blanks following the passage. Use the numbers from the list. (*Note:* Not all types appear in this passage.)

1. Linking
2. Intransitive
3. (Mono)Transitive
4. (Di)Transitive
5. (Complex) Transitive

> To raise money that spring, Margaret's catechism class (1) <u>sold</u> plastic cylinders with a figure of the Virgin Mary inside. They (2) <u>were</u> beige and looked like foot-long rockets. . . . They (3) <u>cost</u> two dollars apiece. Anyone who sold three of them got to name an African Pagan baby who would be baptized by missionaries when the money was sent in. Margaret sold six and [she] (4) <u>named</u> her babies Audrey and Gidget.
> Trudging on Saturday mornings from door to door . . . , Margaret (5) <u>gathered</u> evidence of something she already felt in her bones—that Madrid, where she (6) <u>lived</u>, was not just a gappy little town on the

northern Montana plains. Far from it, it (7) <u>was</u> a place of layers and mysteries, of hidden rooms and muffled dramas. . . .

Selling the rockets, she (8) <u>saw</u> . . . an old man in red boxer shorts vacuuming a carpet. She (9) <u>heard</u> Mr. Badenoch, the meek grade school principal, singing in a heartbreaking voice from beneath a car in his garage, and she (10) <u>watched</u> a three-legged dog with a bow on its collar hop through a tunnel in some bushes. . . .

But this was the most mysterious of all: One morning she (11) <u>knocked</u> lightly on the door of a yellow ranch-style house . . . and heard a woman's distant cry. "So who *are* you anyway? . . . I (12) <u>have</u> no idea," it wailed, "who you could possibly be."

1. __   7. __

2. __   8. __

3. __   9. __

4. __   10. __

5. __   11. __

6. __   12. __

Exercise 6. Recognizing Operator Functions

For these sentences, simplified versions of several in the previous exercise, rewrite them by making them into questions that can be answered by *yes* or *no*. Identify the operator in each by underlining it (see chap. 1 in the textbook, section 1.3.3). Follow the example.

Example: Next spring, Margaret will sell plastic rockets.
Next spring, <u>will</u> Margaret sell plastic rockets?

1. To raise money, Margaret sold plastic cylinders.

_____

2. They were beige.

   Were they beige?

3. They cost two dollars apiece.

_____

4. During that time, Margaret lived in Madrid.

_____

5. Madrid was a place of layers and mysteries.

_____

Exercise 7. Sentence Types

In the following passage, from Ann Tyler's novel *Dinner at the Homesick Restaurant,* indicate the sentence type for the bracketed part of each sentence by writing the corresponding numbers in the blanks following the passage. Use the numbers from the list. (*Note:* In this exercise you are sometimes asked to analyze only the basic part of a sentence. Later chapters will take account of the complete and more complex form that some sentences take.)

1. Linking   (Subject, verb, subject complement)
2. Intransitive   (Subject, verb)
3. (Mono)Transitive   (Subject, verb, direct object)
4. (Di)Transitive   (Subject, verb, indirect object, direct object)
5. (Complex) Transitive (Subject, verb, direct object, object
                          complement)

Because she knew (1) [it would make Ezra happy], she went to visit the restaurant late in the evening. (2) [The rain had stopped], but there was still a mist. . . .(3) [Traffic swished by]; reflections of the headlights wavered on the streets. (4) [The restaurant's kitchen seemed overcrowded]; (5) [it was a miracle] that an acceptable plate of food could emerge from it. (6) [A young girl lifted ladles full of steaming liquid] and emptied them into a bowl. Ezra . . . said, "Why, hello, Jenny," and came to the door where she waited. (7) [Over his jeans he wore a long white apron]; he looked like one of the cooks. He took her around to meet the others; sweaty men chopping or straining or stirring. (8) ["This is my sister, Jenny,"] he would say, but then he'd get sidetracked by some detail and stand there discussing food. (9) ["Can I offer you something to eat?"], he asked finally. "No, (10) [I had supper at home.]"

1. __   4. __   7. __   9. __

2. __   5. __   8. __   10. __

3. __   6. __

Exercise 8. Grammatical Functions

For each underlined structure in this passage from O. Henry's story "A Municipal Report," indicate the grammatical function by writing it in the corresponding blank. Use the abbreviations in the list.

S   (Subject)   SC   (Subject complement)
V   (Verb unit)   OC   (Object complement)
DO   (Direct object)   ADV   (Adverbial)
IO   (Indirect object)

I <u>must tell</u> (1) _____ you how I came to be <u>in Nashville</u> (2), _____ and I assure you <u>the digression</u> (3) _____ brings <u>me</u> (4) _____ <u>much tedium</u> (5) _____, as I'm sure it does you. <u>I</u> (6) _____ was traveling elsewhere on my own business, but I had <u>a commission</u> (7) _____ from a Northern literary magazine to stop over there and establish a personal connection between the publication and one of its contributors, Azalea Adair.

<u>Adair</u> (8) _____ had sent in some essays and poems that had made the editors swear approvingly <u>over their one o'clock luncheon</u> (9) _____. So they <u>had commissioned</u> (10) _____ me to round up said Adair and corner by contract his or her output at two cents a word before some other publisher offered her ten or twenty.

Chapter 2
The Basic Noun Phrase

Exercise 1. Identifying Noun Classes

For the underlined nouns in the following poem, identify each as count or non-count and as abstract or concrete. Be sure to make this identification based on the way in which the noun is used in this particular discourse context. Write your answers in the blanks following the passage. Follow the example.

Example: He drank some (1) <u>coffee</u>.   (1) <u>noncount, concrete</u>

> WHEN I READ SHAKESPEARE—
> *D. H. Lawrence*
>
> When I read Shakespeare I am struck with (1) <u>wonder</u>
> that such trivial people should muse and thunder
> in such lovely (2) <u>language</u>.
>
> Lear, the old buffer, you wonder his (3) <u>daughters</u>
> didn't treat him rougher,
> the (4) <u>chough</u>,[1] the old chuffer!
>
> And Hamlet, how boring, how boring to live with,
> so mean and self-conscious, blowing and snoring
> his wonderful (5) <u>speeches</u>, full of other folks' whoring!
>
> And Macbeth and his (6) <u>Lady</u>, who should have been choring,
> such suburban (7) <u>ambition</u>, so messily goring
> old Duncan with (8) <u>daggers</u>!
>
> How boring, how small Shakespeare's (9) <u>people</u> are!
> Yet the language so lovely! like the dyes from (10) <u>gas-tar</u>.

1. _____, _____   4. _____, _____

2. _____, _____   5. _____, _____

3. _____, _____   6. _____, _____

---

1. chough: a bird of Old World genus, related to crows

7. _____, _____   9. _____, _____

8. _____, _____   10. _____, _____

Exercise 2. Distinguishing Count, Noncount, and Crossover Nouns

Distinguish the underlined nouns as crossover nouns versus nouns that are strictly count or noncount nouns by writing crossover, count, or noncount in the corresponding blanks following the passage (see chap. 2 in the textbook, section 2.2.4). The passage is from Joan Didion's book *Slouching towards Bethlehem*. (*Hint:* As a test for a count noun, try to use the noun in a sentence without an article or a plural; for a noncount noun, try to use it in a sentence as a plural. If the result is a natural sounding sentence and the meanings are the same or closely related, the noun is a crossover noun. Follow the example.)

> *Example:* a. I started a new <u>business</u>./<u>Business</u> is booming.
>   b. <u>Money</u> is scarce./*I need two <u>monies</u>.[2]

Thus (a) is a crossover noun, but (b) is strictly noncount.

> Sometimes I think that those of us who are now in our thirties were born into the last (1) <u>generation</u> to carry the (2) <u>burden</u> of (3) "<u>home</u>," to find in family (4) <u>life</u> the source of all (5) <u>tension</u> and drama. I had by all objective accounts a "normal" and a "happy" family (6) <u>situation</u>, and yet I was almost thirty years old before I could talk to my (7) <u>family</u> on the (8) <u>telephone</u> without crying after I had hung up. We did not fight. Nothing was wrong. And yet some nameless (9) <u>anxiety</u> colored the emotional charges between me and the (10) <u>place</u> that I came from. The (11) <u>question</u> of whether or not you could go home again was a very real part of the sentimental and largely literary (12) <u>baggage</u> with which we left home in the fifties; I suspect that it is irrelevant to the (13) <u>children</u> born of the (14) <u>fragmentation</u> after World (15) <u>War</u> II. . . .

1. _____a_____ abstract   5. _____a_____ abstract

2. _____a_____ abstract   6. _____a_____ abstract

3. _____a_____ concrete/abstract 7. _____a_____ concrete/abstract

4. _____a_____   8. _____a_____ concrete/abstract

---

2. Recall that an asterisk indicates a structure that sounds somewhat odd or incomplete.

9. _b_ abstract   13. _a_ concrete

10. _a_ concrete   14. _a_

11. _a_ abstract   15. _a_ concrete

12. _b_ concrete

Exercise 3. Distinguishing Proper and Common Nouns

In this passage, from "A House of One's Own," by Janet Malcolm, (1) distinguish nouns from adjectives by writing N or ADJ in the corresponding blank in the first column following the passage and (2) distinguish proper nouns from common nouns by writing proper or common in the second column. Follow the example.

> *Example:* She lived near (1) <u>Green</u> (2) <u>Lake</u>.

> 1. <u>ADJ</u>, _____
>
> 2. <u>N</u>, <u>Proper</u>

(*Hint:* Recall from chap. 1 in the textbook the test for noun class membership, *the* _____, and for adjective class membership, *X is very* _____.)

> The legend of (1) <u>Bloomsbury</u>—the tale of how Virginia and (2) <u>Vanessa</u> (3) <u>Stephen</u> emerged from a grim, patriarchal Victorian background to become the pivotal figures in a luminous group of advanced and free-spirited writers and artists—takes its plot from the myth of modernism. (4) <u>Legend</u> and (5) <u>myth</u> alike trace a movement from darkness to light, turgid ugliness to plain beauty, tired realism to vital abstraction, social backwardness to social progress. Virginia Woolf chronicled her and her sister's coming of age in the early years of this century. . . . Virginia, in her memoir (6) "<u>Old</u> (7) <u>Bloomsbury</u>" (1922), recoiled from the suffocating closeness of her childhood home at 22 Hyde Park Gate, in Kensington. In "A (8) <u>Sketch</u> of the (9) <u>Past</u>" Virginia describes "a certain manner" that she and Vanessa were indelibly taught to assume when people came to tea at Hyde Park (10) <u>Gate</u>. "We both learnt the rules of the game of (11) <u>Victorian</u> (12) <u>society</u> so thoroughly that we have never forgotten them," she wrote in 1940. "We still play the game. It is useful."

1. _____, _____   5. _____, _____

2. _____, _____   6. _____, _____

3. _____, _____   7. _____,_____

4. _____, _____   8. _____, _____

9. _____, _____   11. _____, _____

10. _____, _____   12. _____, _____

Exercise 4. Identifying Classes of Determiners

Identify the underlined determiners in the poem "The Wild Swans at Coole" by writing the appropriate numbers in the blanks. Use the numbers in the list. (*Note:* Not all categories necessarily appear in this poem.)

(1) Central determiner
(2) Predeterminer
(3) Postdeterminer
(4) Determiner used as pronominal

THE WILD SWANS AT COOLE
William Butler Yeats

The trees are in their autumn beauty,   1. ___   2. ___
The woodland paths are dry,
Under the October twilight the water
Mirrors a still sky;   3. ___
Upon the brimming water among the stones
Are nine-and-fifty swans.   4. ___

The nineteenth autumn has come upon me   5. ___
Since I first made my count;   6. ___
I saw, before I had well finished,
All suddenly mount   7. ___
And scatter wheeling in great broken rings
upon their clamorous wings.   8. ___

I have looked upon those brilliant creatures,   9. |___
and now my heart is sore.
All's changed since I, hearing at twilight,
The first time on this shore,   10. ___   11. ___
The bell-beat of their wings above my head,
Trod with a lighter tread.

Unwearied still, lover by lover,
They paddle in the cold   12. ___
Companionable streams or climb the air;

<u>Their</u> hearts have not grown old;   13. ___
Passion or conquest, wander where they will,
Attend upon them still.

But now they drift on <u>the</u> still water,   14. ___
Mysterious, beautiful;
Among what rushes will they build,
By what lake's edge or pool
Delight men's eyes when I awake <u>some</u> day   15. ___
To find they have flown away?

Exercise 5. Using Definite and Indefinite Determiners

Fill in the blanks in the following paragraph, from W. Somerset Maugham's "The Outstation," by using the most appropriate determiner from the list. (If you choose the zero determiner, simply leave the space blank.) You may use a determiner more than once. In some cases, more than one choice may be possible.

In choosing which determiner to use, first read the passage and try to make your choice based on the point of view you think the author is inviting the reader to assume. For example, try to determine how much information we are to assume as a shared perspective of familiar surroundings or how much as an unshared one of unfamiliar surroundings. Remember also that some information is assumed to be familiar based on the context of the passage itself.

the	this	his	some
a	that	my	any
an	these	our	little
	those	their	few

The new assistant arrived in the afternoon. When the Resident, Mr. Warburton, was told that the prahu was in sight he put on his solar topee and went down to (1) _____ landing-stage. From the landing-stage he watched (2) _____ bend of the river round which in (3) _____ moment (4) _____ boat would sweep. He looked very smart in (5) _____ spotless ducks and white shoes. He held under (6) _____ arm a gold-headed Malacca cane which had been given him by (7) _____ Sultan of Perak. He awaited (8) _____ newcomer with (9) _____ mingled

feelings. . . . He had been so long (10) _____ only white man

there that he could not face (11) _____ arrival of another with-

out (12) _____ misgiving. He was accustomed to (13) _____

_____ loneliness. During (14) _____ war he had not seen

(15) _____ English face for three years; and once when he was

instructed to put up (16) _____ afforestation officer he was

seized with panic, so that when (17) _____ stranger was due

to arrive, having arranged everything for (18) _____ reception,

he wrote (19) _____ note telling him he was obliged to go up-

river, and fled; he remained away till he was informed by a messenger

that (20) _____ guest had left.

Exercise 6. Using Definite Articles with Count and Noncount Nouns

In this passage, from David Guterson's novel *Snow Falling on Cedars,* the underlined nouns can all appear with the definite article. First, identify those nouns
that can also be used with an indefinite article by writing indefinite in the corresponding blank following the passage. Next, for those that cannot easily be
used in a natural sounding way with the indefinite article, give a brief explana-
tion in the space following.

Snow fell that (1) <u>morning</u> outside the courthouse windows, four tall,
narrow arches of leaded (2) <u>glass</u> that yielded a great quantity of weak
December light. A wind from the (3) <u>sea</u> lofted and ran toward the ease-
ments. Beyond the courthouse the town of Amity Harbor spread along
the island (4) <u>shoreline</u>. A few wind-whipped and decrepit Victorian
mansions, remnants of a lost era of seagoing (5) <u>optimism</u>, loomed out
of the snowfall on the town's sporadic hills. Beyond them, cedars wove
a steep mat of still green. The (6) <u>snow</u> blurred from vision the clean
contours of these cedar hills. The sea wind drove snowflakes steadily in-
land, hurling them against the fragrant trees. . . .

    The accused (7) <u>man</u>, with one segment of his (8) <u>consciousness</u>,
watched the falling snow outside the windows. He had been exiled in
the county (9) <u>jail</u> for seventy-seven days—the last (10) <u>part</u> of Sep-

tember, all of October and all of November, the first (11) <u>week</u> of December in jail. There was no window anywhere in his basement (12) <u>cell</u>, no portal through which the autumn light could come to him. He had missed autumn, he realized now—it had passed already, evaporated. The snowfall . . . struck him as infinitely beautiful.

1. _____   7. _____

2. _____   8. _____

3. _____   9. _____

4. _____   10. _____

5. _____   11. _____

6. _____   12. _____

Exercise 7. Determiner Functions in Discourse

Read the following passage, paying particular attention to the underlined noun phrases and their functions in contributing to the point of view the author seems to be establishing. The passage is the introductory paragraph of Conrad Aiken's short story "Impulse."

Based on the nature of these noun phrases, decide which of the following best describes the perspective the author seems to be inviting the reader to take. Write the number of your answer on the line at the end of the passage. Be prepared to defend your answer.

Perspective

(1) Unfamiliar: Known to narrator; unknown to reader, who is being told of the scene for the first time

(2) Unfamiliar: Shared with narrator (or character); unknown to both narrator (or character) and reader, who are sharing the scene for the first time

(3) Familiar: Shared with narrator (or character); known to both narrator (or character) and reader

Michael Lowes hummed as he shaved, amused by the face he saw—the pallid, asymmetrical face, with the right eye so much higher than the left, and its eyebrow so peculiarly arched, like a "v" turned upside down. Perhaps this day wouldn't be as bad as the last. In fact, he knew it wouldn't be, and that was why he hummed. This was the bi-weekly day of escape, when he would stay out for the evening, and play bridge with Hurwitz, Bryant, and Smith. Should he tell Dora at the breakfast table? No, better not. Particularly in view of last night's row about unpaid bills. And there would be more of them, probably, beside his plate. The rent. The coal. The doctor who had attended to the children. Jeez, what a life. Maybe it was time to do a new jump. And Dora was beginning to get restless again.

Perspective ___

Exercise 8. More on Determiner Functions

Read the following passage, paying careful attention to the underlined noun phrases and their functions in contributing to the point of view the author seems to be establishing. The passage is the introductory paragraph of Henry James's novel *Daisy Miller.*

Based on the nature of these noun phrases, decide which of the following best describes the perspective the author seems to be inviting the reader to take. Write the number of your answer on the line at the end of the passage. Be prepared to defend your answer.

Perspective

    (1) Unfamiliar: Known to narrator; unknown to reader, who is being told of the scene for the first time

    (2) Unfamiliar: Shared with narrator (or character); unknown to both narrator (or character) and reader, who are sharing the scene for the first time

    (3) Familiar: Shared with narrator (or character); known to both narrator (or character) and reader

    At the little town of Vevey, in Switzerland, there is a particularly comfortable hotel. There are, indeed, many hotels; for the entertainment of tourists is the business of the place, which, as many travellers will remember, is seated upon the edge of a remarkably blue lake—a lake that it behooves every tourist to visit. The shore of the lake presents an unbroken array of establishments of this order, of every category, from the "grand hotel" of the newest fashion, with a chalk-white front, a hundred balconies, and a dozen flags flying from its roof, to the little Swiss pension of an elder day, with its name inscribed in German-looking lettering upon a pink or yellow wall, and an awkward summer-house in the angle of the garden. One of the hotels in Vevey, however, is famous, even classical, being distinguished from many of its upstart neighbors by an air both of luxury and of maturity. In this region, in the month of June, American travellers are extremely numerous; it may be said, indeed, that Vevey assumes at this period some of the characteristics of an American watering-place.

Perspective ___

Chapter 3
Adjectives, Adverbs, and Adverbials

Exercise 1. Adjective Functions: Attributive and Predicative

In the following passage, from Thomas Kuhn's article "The Historical Structure of Scientific Discovery," identify the syntactic function of each underlined adjective as central (C), attributive only (A), or predicative only (P) by writing the appropriate letters in the blanks following the passage.

You can test these adjectives by trying them out in the opposite syntactic slots; if they can appear in both slots, they are central; if not, they are limited to the slot in which they appear, as either attributive only or predicative only. If you are a native speaker, you can trust your own intuitions to tell you the possible slots for each in English. For instance, the adjective in "a clear example" can also appear in "the example is clear" and is, therefore, a central adjective. However, in "an early example," the adjective cannot appear in the predicative slot, "*the example is early," and is thus attributive only.

> One of the few (1) historical elements recurrent in the textbooks from which the (2) prospective scientist learns his field is the attribution of particular (3) natural phenomena to the historical personages who first discovered them. As a result of this and other aspects of their training, discovery becomes for many scientists an (4) important goal. (5) Professional prestige is often closely associated with these acquisitions. (6) Small wonder, then, that (7) acrimonious disputes about priority and independence in discovery have often marred the normally (8) placid tenor of scientific communication. . . . Many scientific discoveries are not the sort of event about which the questions "Where?" and . . . "When?" can appropriately be asked. [The asking of these questions] is (9) symptomatic of a (10) fundamental inappropriateness in our image of discovery.

1. __   4. __   7. __   9. __

2. __   5. __   8. __   10. __

3. __   6. __

Exercise 2. Adverbs: Syntactic Functions

In this paragraph, from Henry James's novel *Daisy Miller*, identify the underlined adverbs according to syntactic function by writing the appropriate numbers in the blanks. Use the numbers in the list.

(1) Premodifier of adjective
(2) Premodifier of adverb
(3) Adverbial

Follow the example.

Example: _3_ The train is moving <u>fast</u>.

"Who is Giovanelli?"

"The little Italian. I have asked questions about him and learned something. He is (1) <u>apparently</u> a (2) <u>perfectly</u> respectable little man. I believe he is in a small way a *cavaliere avocato*. But he doesn't move in what are called the first circles. I think it is (3) <u>really</u> not (4) <u>absolutely</u> impossible that the courier introduced him. He is (5) <u>evidently</u> (6) <u>immensely</u> charmed with Miss Miller. If she thinks him the finest gentleman in the world, he, on his side, has (7) <u>never</u> found himself in personal contact with such splendour, such opulence, such expensiveness as this young lady's. And (8) <u>then</u> she must seem to him (9) <u>wonderfully</u> pretty and interesting. I rather doubt that he dreams of marrying her. That must appear to him (10) <u>too</u> impossible a piece of luck. He has nothing but his handsome face to offer, and there is a substantial Mr. Miller in that mysterious land of dollars."

1. ___   6. ___

2. ___   7. ___

3. ___   8. ___

4. ___   9. ___

5. ___   10. ___

Exercise 3. Identifying Adjective and Adverb Forms

In this passage, from *Journal of a Solitude,* by May Sarton, first identify the underlined word as an adjective (ADJ) or as an adverb (ADV). Then decide which adjectives and adverbs can be identified strictly according to characteristics of form, that is, according to suffixes found only with adjectives or only with adverbs, versus those that cannot be identified according to a characteristic of form. For those that can be identified according to form alone, write the suffix for that adjective or adverb in the corresponding blank following the passage. Otherwise, leave the space blank. Follow the example.

	ADJ/ADV	Suffix
Example: (i) good	ADJ	_____
(ii) childlike	ADJ	-like _____

In a period of (1) <u>happy</u> and (2) <u>fruitful</u> isolation such as this, any interruption, any intrusion of the social, any obligation breaks the thread on my loom, breaks the pattern. Two nights ago I was called at the (3) <u>last</u> minute to attend the caucus of Town Meeting . . . and it threw me. But at least the companionship gave me one insight: a neighbor told me that she had been in a (4) <u>small</u> car accident and had managed to persuade the local paper to ignore her (5) <u>true</u> age (as it appears on her license) and to print her age as thirty-nine! I was (6) <u>really</u> astonished by this confidence. I am (7) <u>proud</u> of being fifty-eight, and (8) <u>still</u> alive and kicking, in love, more (9) <u>creative</u>, balanced, and potent than I have (10) <u>ever</u> been. I mind certain (11) <u>physical</u> deteriorations, but not really. And not at all when I look at the (12) <u>marvelous</u> photograph that Bill sent me of Isak Dinesen just (13) <u>before</u> she died. For after all we make our faces as we go along, and who when (14) <u>young</u> could ever look as she does? The (15) <u>ineffable</u> sweetness of the smile, the total acceptance and joy one receives from it, life, death, everything taken in and, as it were, savored—and let go.

	ADJ/ADV	Suffix
1. happy	Adj	_____
2. fruitful	Adj.	-ful _____
3. last	_____	_____
4. small	Adj.	_____
5. true	_____	_____
6. really	Adv.	_____
7. proud	Adj.	_____

8. still   _____   _____

9. creative   _____   _____

10. ever   _____   _____

11. physical   _____   _____

12. marvelous   _____   _____

13. before   _____   _____

14. young   _____   _____

15. ineffable   _____   _____

Exercise 4. Adverbials

In this passage, from Janet Malcolm's essay "A House of One's Own," repeated from chapter 2 in this workbook, (1) identify the type of structure as an adverb (ADV), a prepositional phrase (PP), or a noun phrase (NP) and (2) identify the category of each adverb, prepositional phrase, or noun phrase as one of the following types. Write your answers in the blanks following the passage.

Time   Degree
Place: direction   Manner
Place: location   Frequency
Place: source   Viewpoint
Place: goal   Limiter

Follow the example.

> *Example:* She would be (1) <u>there</u> (2) <u>all day.</u>
>   1. <u>ADV</u>, <u>Place: location</u>
>   2. <u>NP</u>, <u>Time</u>

> The legend of Bloomsbury—the tale of how Virginia and Vanessa Stephen emerged (1) <u>from a grim, patriarchal Victorian background</u> to become the pivotal figures in a luminous group of advanced and free-spirited writers and artists—takes its plot (2) <u>from the myth</u> of modernism. Legend and myth alike trace a movement (3) <u>from darkness</u> (4) <u>to light,</u> turgid ugliness to plain beauty, tired realism to vital abstraction, social backwardness to social progress. Virginia Woolf chronicled her and her sister's coming of age (5) <u>in the early years</u> of this century. . . . Vir-

ginia, (6) <u>in her memoir "Old Bloomsbury"</u> (1922), recoiled from the suffocating closeness of her childhood home (7) <u>at 22 Hyde Park Gate</u>, (8) <u>in Kensington</u>. (9) <u>In "A Sketch of the Past"</u> Virginia describes "a certain manner" that she and Vanessa were (10) <u>indelibly</u> taught to assume when people came to tea at Hyde Park Gate. "We both learnt the rules of the game of Victorian society (11) <u>so</u> (12) <u>thoroughly</u> that we have (13) <u>never</u> forgotten them," she wrote (14) <u>in 1940</u>. "We (15) <u>still</u> play the game. It is useful."

functioning as adverbial phrase

1. PP. , direction   9. ____ , ____

2. Adv. , viewpoint   10. ____ , ____

3. ____ , ____   11. ____ , ____

4. ____ , ____   12. ____ , ____

5. Adv , time   13. ____ , ____

6. ____ , ____   14. ____ , ____

7. ____ , ____   15. ____ , ____

8. ____ , ____

Exercise 5. Distinguishing Adjective and Adverb Functions

In this poem, decide whether each underlined word functions as an adjective (ADJ) or an adverb (ADV). Indicate which by writing either ADJ or ADV in the corresponding blank following the poem.

A CONSIDERABLE SPECK
Robert Frost

A speck that would have been beneath my sight
On any but a paper sheet (1) <u>so</u> (2) <u>white</u>
Set off across what I had written (3) <u>there</u>.
And I had (4) <u>idly</u> poised my pen in air
To stop it with a period of ink
When something (5) <u>strange</u> about it made me think.
This was no dust speck by my breathing blown,
But (6) <u>unmistakably</u> a living mite
With inclinations it could call its own.
It paused as with suspicion of my pen,

And then came (7) <u>wildly</u> racing on again
To where my manuscript was not yet (8) <u>dry</u>;
Then paused again and either drank or smelt—
With loathing, for again it turned to fly.
(9) <u>Plainly</u> with an intelligence I dealt.
It seemed (10) <u>too</u> (11) <u>tiny</u> to have room for feet,
Yet must have had a set of them (12) <u>complete</u>
To express (13) <u>how</u> much it didn't want to die.
It ran with terror and with cunning crept.
It faltered: I could see it hesitate;
(14) <u>Then</u> in the middle of the open sheet
Cower down in desperation to accept
Whatever I accorded it of fate.
I have none of the tenderer-than-thou
(15) <u>Collectivistic</u> regimenting love
With which the modern world is being swept.
But this (16) <u>poor</u> (17) <u>microscopic</u> item now!
Since it was nothing I knew evil of
I let it lie (18) <u>there</u> till I hope it slept.
I have a mind myself and recognize
Mind when I meet with it in any guise.
No one can know (19) <u>how</u> glad I am to find
On any sheet the (20) <u>least</u> display of mind.

1. _____   6. _____   11. _____   16. _____

2. _____   7. _____   12. _____   17. _____

3. _____   8. _____   13. _____   18. _____

4. _____   9. _____   14. _____   19. _____

5. _____   10. _____   15. _____   20. _____

Exercise 6. More on Adjective and Adverb Functions

In this passage, from Loren Eiseley's essay "The Brown Wasps," decide whether each underlined word functions as an adjective (ADJ) or an adverb (ADV). Indicate which by writing either ADJ or ADV in the corresponding blank following the passage.

There is a corner in the waiting room of one of the great (1) <u>Eastern</u> stations where women never sit. It is (2) <u>always</u> in the shadow and overhung by rows of lockers. It is, however, always frequented—not so much by (3) <u>genuine</u> travelers as by the dying. It is here that a (4) <u>certain</u> element of the abandoned poor seeks a refuge out of the weather, clinging for a few hours longer to the city that has fathered them. In a (5) <u>precisely</u> (6) <u>similar</u> manner I have seen, on a (7) <u>sunny</u> day in midwinter, a few (8) <u>old</u> (9) <u>brown</u> wasps creep slowly over an abandoned wasp nest in a thicket. Numbed and forgetful and frost-blackened, the hum of the spring hive still resounded (10) <u>faintly</u> in their (11) <u>sodden</u> tissues. Then the temperature would fall and they would drop away into the (12) <u>white</u> oblivion of the snow. Here in the station it is in no way (13) <u>different</u> save that the city is (14) <u>busy</u> in its snows. But the old ones cling to their seats as though these were (15) <u>symbolic</u> and could not be given up. Now and then they sleep, their gray old heads resting with (16) <u>painful</u> awkwardness on the backs of the benches. . . . Then a policeman comes by on his round and nudges them (17) <u>upright</u>.

"You can't sleep here," he growls.

A strange ritual then begins. An old man is (18) <u>difficult</u> to waken. After a muttered conversation the policeman presses a coin into his hand and passes (19) <u>fiercely</u> along the benches prodding and gesturing toward the door. . . . One man, after a (20) <u>slight</u>, (21) <u>apologetic</u> lurch, does not move at all. (22) <u>Tubercularly</u> (23) <u>thin</u>, he sleeps on (24) <u>steadily</u>. The policeman does not look back. To him, too, this has become a ritual. He will not have to notice it again (25) <u>officially</u> for another hour.

1. _____	6. _____	11. _____	16. _____	21. _____
2. _____	7. _____	12. _____	17. _____	22. _____
3. _____	8. _____	13. _____	18. _____	23. _____
4. _____	9. _____	14. _____	19. _____	24. _____
5. _____	10. _____	15. _____	20. _____	25. _____

Exercise 7. Ambiguities of Form and Function

Consider the function of the word *perhaps* in e. e. cummings's poem "Spring is like a perhaps hand." Then answer the questions that follow.

Spring is like a perhaps hand
(which comes carefully
out of Nowhere)arranging

a window,into which people look(while
people stare
arranging and changing placing
carefully there a strange
thing and a known thing here)and

changing everything carefully

spring is like a perhaps
Hand in a window
(carefully to
and fro moving New and
Old things,while
people stare carefully
moving a perhaps
fraction of flower here placing
an inch of air there)and

without breaking anything.

1. In ordinary usage, what is the syntactic function of *perhaps?* That is, is it an adjective, an adverb premodifier, or an adverbial?

2. As *perhaps* is used in this poem, what is a second possible syntactic function in the phrases *a perhaps hand* and *a perhaps fraction of flower?*

3. What syntactic clues help in finding an answer to question 2?

4. Can you think of ways in which this ambiguous usage might invite a new perspective on how we view spring? On our perception of the metaphor *the hand of Spring?*

Exercise 8. Morphology: Roots and Affixes

In the following passage, from the essay "Soft Soap and the Nitty-Gritty," by Robert M. Adams, which also appears in chapter 3 in the textbook, examine each underlined word to determine the root. Write it in the corresponding blank following the passage. Follow the example.

Example: unhealthy   root: health

You could call euphemism the (1) deodorant of language. . . . The social (2) sciences, which for (3) years have been trying to develop a sanitized, neutral, and (4) <u>preferably</u> artificial vocabulary, serve as a major source of supply. "Senior citizens," for example, is a standard euphemism for the old. . . . (5) "<u>Upwardly</u> mobile" is a (6) <u>similarly</u> sanitized form of "ambitious." . . . Foreign languages used to, and (7) <u>occasionally</u> still do, provide evasion (8) <u>devices</u>. Latin was (9) <u>retained</u> in (10) <u>transla-tions</u> of ancient (11) <u>texts</u> when one (12) <u>wanted</u> the (13) <u>reader</u> to work so hard (14) <u>deciphering</u> it that all obscene (15) <u>pleasures</u> would be oblit-erated by the labor of translation.

prefix 'odor'

1. <u>Suffix- deriv.</u>
2. <u>Suffix- inflect</u>
3. <u>Suffix - inflect</u>
4. <u>Suffix- deriv.</u>
5. <u>Suffix</u> *derivational*
6. <u>Suffix -deriv.</u>
7. <u>Suffix- deriv.</u>
8. <u>suffix -inflect.</u>
9. <u>suffix- inflect.</u>
10. <u>suffix -inflect.</u>
11. <u>suffix - inflect.</u>
12. <u>Suffix- inflect.</u>
13. <u>Suffix - deriv.</u>
14. *prefix* <u>Suffix- deriv.</u>
15. <u>suffix - deriv.</u>

Exercise 9. Morphology: Compounding

The following passage is from Diane Johnson's short story "Great Barrier Reef." For each underlined word, decide if it is a <u>compound</u> word (the combination of two free morphemes) or if it is a word composed of a single root and one or more affixes. Mark yes in the first column following the passage if it is a com-pound and no in the second column if it is not; then write the syntactic func-tion for each word, according to its use in the context in which it appears. Use the abbreviations in the list. Follow the example.

ADJ (Adjective)
ADV (Adverb)
N (Noun)
V (Verb)

		Yes	No	Syntactic Function
Example: a <u>lighthouse</u>	(1)	X	__	N
a <u>sailor</u> hat	(2)	__	X	ADJ

(1) <u>Statuettes</u> of drunken sailors, velvet pictures of island (2) <u>maid-ens</u>, plastic (3) <u>seashell</u> lamps made in Taiwan. What contempt the people who think up souvenirs have for other people! . . .

Each morning, each (4) <u>afternoon</u>, we stopped at another island.

This one was (5) <u>Daydream</u> Island. "It's lovely, isn't it, dear?" Priscilla said to me. "People like to see a bit of a new place, the (6) <u>shopping</u>, they have different things to make it interesting." But it wasn't different, it was the same each day: the crew hands the heavy, (7) <u>sacklike</u> people, grunting, down into (8) <u>rowboats</u>, and hauls them out onto a (9) <u>sandy</u> slope of beach. Up they trudge toward a souvenir shop. This one had large shells perched on legs, and small shells pasted in designs . . . , and (10) <u>earrings</u> made of shells. . . .

"I don't care, I do hate [such people]," I ranted (11) <u>passionately</u> to J. . . . They're ugly (12) <u>consumers</u>, they can't look at a shell (13) <u>unless</u> it's (14) <u>coated</u> in plastic, they never look at the sea—why are they here? Why don't they stay in Perth and Adelaide?—you can buy shells there, and (15) <u>swizzlesticks</u> in the shape of hula girls." Of course J. hadn't an answer for this, of course I was right.

	Yes	*No*	*Syntactic Function*
1.	___	___	_____
2.	___	___	_____
3.	___	___	_____
4.	___	___	_____
5.	___	___	_____
6.	___	___	_____
7.	___	___	_____
8.	___	___	_____
9.	___	___	_____
10.	___	___	_____
11.	___	___	_____
12.	___	___	_____
13.	___	___	_____
14.	___	___	_____
15.	___	___	_____

Chapter 4

The Basic Verb Phrase

Exercise 1. Verb Forms

Identify the form of each underlined (lexical) verb in the following passage by writing the appropriate symbol from the left column of the list in the corresponding blank at the end. The passage is from *I Know Why the Caged Bird Sings,* by Maya Angelou.

V	(Base form)
V–s	(*-s* form)
V–ed	(Past form)
V–ing	(*-ing* participle form)
V–en	(*-en* participle form)

Entering Stamps, I (1) <u>had</u> the feeling that I was (2) <u>stepping</u> over the borderlines of the map of the world and would fall . . . right off the end of the world. . . .

For an indeterminate time nothing was (3) <u>demanded</u> of me or Bailey. We (4) <u>were</u>, after all, Mrs. Henderson's California grandchildren, and had (5) <u>been</u> away on a glamorous trip way up North to the fabulous St. Louis. . . . Farmers and maids, cooks and handymen, carpenters and all the children in town (6) <u>made</u> regular pilgrimages to the Store. "Just to see the travelers." They (7) <u>stood</u> around like cutout cardboard figures and asked, "Well, how (8) <u>is</u> it up North?"

Bailey (9) <u>took</u> it upon himself to answer every question. . . . "They have, in the North, buildings so high that for months, in the winter, you can't (10) <u>see</u> the top floors. . . . They've (11) <u>got</u> watermelons twice the size of a cow's head and sweeter than syrup. . . . And if you can (12) <u>count</u> the watermelon's seeds, before it is (13) <u>cut</u> open, you can win five zillion dollars and a new car. . . . Everybody (14) <u>wears</u> new clothes and has inside toilets. If you (15) <u>fall</u> down in one of them, you get flushed away into the Mississippi River."

1. _____   3. _____   5. _____

2. _____   4. _____   6. _____

7. _____   10. _____   13. _____

8. _____   11. _____   14. _____

9. _____   12. _____   15. _____

Exercise 2. Distinguishing Regular and Irregular Verbs

Identify the underlined verbs as either regular or irregular by writing R or I in the corresponding blanks at the end. The passage is from the opening paragraphs of Ursula K. LeGuin's novel *The Lathe of Heaven*. If you are a native speaker of English, you should be able to "test" these verbs by using them in a sentence with past tense and with perfect aspect. Follow the example.

> *Example:* (i) *tug:* "The wave *tugged* the jellyfish then; the wave *has tugged* the jellyfish before." Since both have the regular *-ed* ending, the verb is regular.
>
> (ii) *drive:* "The waves *drove* the jellyfish toward the sandy shore then; the waves *have driven* them there many times before." Since both have irregular forms, not *-ed,* the verb is irregular.

Current-borne, wave-flung, tugged hugely by the whole might of ocean, the jellyfish (1) <u>drifts</u> in the tidal abyss. The light (2) <u>shines</u> through it, and the dark (3) <u>enters</u> it. Borne, flung, tugged from anywhere to anywhere, for in the deep sea there (4) <u>is</u> no compass but nearer and farther, higher and lower, the jellyfish (5) <u>hangs</u> and (6) <u>sways</u>; pulses (7) <u>move</u> slight and quick within it, as the vast diurnal pulses (8) <u>beat</u> in the moondriven sea. Hanging, swaying, pulsing, the most vulnerable and insubstantial creature, it (9) <u>has</u> for its defense the violence and power of the whole ocean, to which it has entrusted its being, its going, and its will.

But here (10) <u>rise</u> the stubborn continents. The shelves of gravel and the cliffs of rock (11) <u>break</u> from water baldly into air, that dry, terrible outerspace of radiance and instability, where there is no support for life. And now, now the currents (12) <u>mislead</u>, and the waves (13) <u>betray</u>, breaking their endless circle, to (14) <u>leap</u> up in loud foam against rock and air, breaking.

What will the creature made all of seadrift (15) <u>do</u> on the dry sand of daylight; what will the mind do, each morning, waking?

1. __   3. __

2. __   4. __

5. __   11. __

6. __   12. __

7. __   13. __

8. __   14. __

9. __   15. __

10. __

Exercise 3. Identifying Forms of Regular and Irregular Verbs

Consider again the verbs in the passage from Ursula K. LeGuin's *The Lathe of Heaven*. For each verb, write the past form and the *-en* participle form in the blanks following the passage by using the same test suggested in exercise 2 for regular and irregular verbs.

Current-borne, wave-flung, tugged hugely by the whole might of ocean, the jellyfish (1) <u>drifts</u> in the tidal abyss. The light (2) <u>shines</u> through it, and the dark (3) <u>enters</u> it. Borne, flung, tugged from anywhere to anywhere, for in the deep sea there (4) <u>is</u> no compass but nearer and farther, higher and lower, the jellyfish (5) <u>hangs</u> and (6) <u>sways</u>; pulses (7) <u>move</u> slight and quick within it, as the vast diurnal pulses (8) <u>beat</u> in the moondriven sea. Hanging, swaying, pulsing, the most vulnerable and insubstantial creature, it (9) <u>has</u> for its defense the violence and power of the whole ocean, to which it has entrusted its being, its going, and its will.

But here (10) <u>rise</u> the stubborn continents. The shelves of gravel and the cliffs of rock (11) <u>break</u> from water baldly into air, that dry, terrible outerspace of radiance and instability, where there is no support for life. And now, now the currents (12) <u>mislead</u>, and the waves (13) <u>betray</u>, breaking their endless circle, to (14) <u>leap</u> up in loud foam against rock and air, breaking.

What will the creature made all of seadrift (15) <u>do</u> on the dry sand of daylight; what will the mind do, each morning, waking?

Past Form   *-En Participle Form*

1. _____   _____

2. _____   _____

3. _____   _____

4. _____   _____

5. _____   _____

6. _____   _____

7. _____   _____

8. _____   _____

9. _____   _____

10. _____   _____

11. _____   _____

12. _____   _____

13. _____   _____

14. _____   _____

15. _____   _____

Exercise 4. Tense and Aspect

In the following passage, from Annie Dillard's *Pilgrim at Tinker's Creek,* identify each underlined verb phrase unit by writing the corresponding letters in the blanks following the passage. Use the letters in the list. (*Note:* Not all of the forms listed necessarily appear in the passage.)

a. Simple present   e. Present perfect
b. Simple past   f. Past perfect
c. Present progressive   g. Present perfect progressive
d. Past progressive   h. Past perfect progressive

I (1) [had been] ambling across this hill [for several hours] that day, when [suddenly] I (2) noticed a speck of pure white. . . . I (3) leaned to examine the white thing and saw a mass of bubbles like spittle. Then I (4) saw something dark like an engorged leech rummaging over the spittle, and then I saw the praying mantis. . . .

The male (5) was nowhere in sight. The female (6) had probably eaten him. Fabre says that, at least in captivity, the female will mate with and devour up to seven males, whether she (7) has laid her egg cases or not. The mating rites of mantises (8) are well known: a chemical produced in the head of the male insect (9) says, in effect, "No, (10) don't go near her, you fool, she'll eat you alive." At the same time a chemical in his abdomen says, "Yes, by all means, now and forever yes."

While the male (11) is making up what passes for his mind, the female (12) tips the balance in her favor by eating his head. Fabre (13) describes the mating . . . as follows: "The male, absorbed in the performance of his vital functions, (14) holds the female in a tight embrace. But the wretch (15) has no head; he has no neck; he has hardly a body."

1. ___   6. ___   11. ___

2. ___   7. ___   12. ___

3. ___   8. ___   13. ___

4. ___   9. ___   14. ___

5. ___   10. ___   15. ___

Exercise 5. Auxiliaries and Tense

The verb phrases underlined in this passage include both primary auxiliaries *(have, be)* and modal auxiliaries. Examine the verb phrase units and identify the tense or aspect by writing the corresponding letters in the blanks following the passage. Use the letters in the list. The excerpt is from the Ambrose Bierce story "An Occurrence at Owl Creek Bridge."

a. Simple present   e. Present perfect
b. Simple past   f. Past perfect
c. Present progressive   g. Present perfect progressive
d. Past progressive   h. Past perfect progressive

The man who (1) was engaged in being hanged was apparently about thirty-five years of age. He was a civilian, if one (2) might judge from his dress, which was that of a planter. . . . The preparations being complete, the two private soldiers stepped aside and each drew the plank upon which he (3) had been standing.

[The man] closed his eyes in order to fix his last thoughts upon his wife and children. The water, touched to gold by the early sun, the brooding mists . . . all (4) had distracted him. And now he became conscious of a new disturbance. Striking through the thought of his dear ones was a sound which he (5) could neither ignore nor understand, a sharp, distinct, metallic percussion like the stroke of a blacksmith's hammer upon the anvil. . . . [It] hurt his ears; he feared he (6) <u>would</u> <u>shriek</u>. What he heard was the ticking of his watch.

He unclosed his eyes and saw again the water below him. "If I (7) <u>could</u> <u>free</u> my hands," he thought, "I (8) <u>might</u> <u>throw</u> off the noose and spring into the stream. By diving I (9) <u>could</u> <u>evade</u> the bullets, and, swimming vigorously, reach the bank, take to the woods, and get away home. . . ."

As these thoughts . . . (10) <u>were</u> <u>flashed</u> into the doomed man's brain rather than evolved from it, the captain nodded to the sergeant. The sergeant stepped aside.

As Peyton Farquhar fell straight downward through the bridge, he lost consciousness and was as one already dead. . .Then, all at once, with terrible suddenness, the power of thought (11) <u>was</u> <u>restored</u>; he knew that the rope (12) <u>had</u> <u>broken</u> and he (13) <u>had</u> <u>fallen</u> into the stream. . . . He (14) <u>was</u> still <u>sinking</u>, for the light became fainter and fainter. Then it began to grow and brighten, and he knew that he (15) <u>was</u> <u>rising</u> toward the surface.

1. __	6. __	11. __
2. __	7. __	12. __
3. __	8. __	13. __
4. __	9. __	14. __
5. __	10. __	15. __

Exercise 6. Passive Voice

Identify the underlined verb units as active voice or as passive voice by writing active or passive in the blanks in the first column following the passage. Then identify the tense or aspect of the verb in the second column by choosing the corresponding letter from the list. (*Note:* Not all of the forms listed necessarily appear in the passage.) The passage is from Ken Kesey's novel *Sometimes a Great Notion*.

a. Simple present   e. Present perfect
b. Simple past   f. Past perfect
c. Present progressive   g. Present perfect progressive
d. Past progressive   h. Past perfect progressive

They (1) <u>have been drinking</u> and discussing since early afternoon . . . and, while they (2) <u>formed</u> no official organization, this casual group of eight or ten citizens, they (3) <u>were</u> nevertheless <u>recognized</u> as the ruling body of the town's opinion and their decisions (4) <u>were</u> <u>sanctified,</u> as was the hall where they met. . . .

This hall, the Snag Saloon, is a few doors down from the movie-show house and across the street from the grange hall. . . . The wide front window (5) <u>contains</u> an assortment of neon signs that (6) <u>have been collected</u> from the fronts of numerous competing bars that Teddy (7) <u>has forced</u> out of business over the years. . . .

Yet, The Snag, which boasts a score of banners, has no sign of its own. Years ago the words *Snag Saloon & Grill* (8) <u>had been painted</u> on to the greened glass of the windows, but as Teddy began buying other bars and closing them, he scraped off more and more of the green to make room for the captured neons which he flaunted like enemy scalps. . . .

There is one sign, however, that (9) <u>is afforded</u> individual distinction. . . . "*Remember . . . One Drink Is Too Many. WCTU.*"

A short, plump polyp of man in a land of rangy loggers, Teddy (10) <u>is appeased</u> by his collection of signs. . . . It was these symbols of success that proved his size.

Voice	*Tense or Aspect*
1. _active_	—
2. _active_	—
3. _passive_	—
4. _passive_	past tense
5. _active_	present
6. _passive_	—
7. _active_	—
8. _passive_	past perfect
9. _passive_	present
10. _passive_	present

Exercise 7. Discourse Functions of Tense and Aspect

Read the following passage, from John Cheever's story "Goodbye, My Brother," noting the chronological order of events as expressed by the underlined tense and aspect forms and their sequencing, which, together with adverbials, help us keep track of events in the discourse. Then make a list of the events in the order in which they occur, as follows.

A. As a starting point, use the time frame of the verb *said* in the first line, which anchors us on a day in the narrator's past, and list the events as they unfolded on that day.
B. Make a separate list of events that occurred before that day, again in the order in which they occurred.
C. For any simultaneous events, list them together on the same line.

Base your list only on the events indicated by the underlined verb phrases.

"I don't like it here," [Lawrence] said bluntly, without raising his eyes. "I'm going to sell my equity in the house to Chaddy. . . . The only reason I came back was to say goodbye."

I let him get ahead and I walked behind him, looking at his shoulders and thinking of all the goodbyes he had made. When Father drowned, he went to the church and said goodbye to Father. It was only three years later that he concluded that Mother was frivolous and said goodbye to her. In his freshman year at college, he had been good friends with his roommate, but the man drank too much, and at the beginning of the spring term Lawrence changed roommates and said goodbye to his friend. When he had been in college for two years, he concluded that the atmosphere was too sequestered and he said goodbye to Yale. He enrolled at Columbia and got his law degree there, but he found his first employer dishonest, and at the end of six months he said goodbye to a good job. He married Ruth in City Hall and said goodbye to the Protestant Episcopal Church; they went to live on a back street in Tuckahoe and said goodbye to the middle class. . . .

"You're a gloomy son of a bitch," I said.

"Get your face out of mine," he said. He walked along.

Then I picked up a root and, coming at his back, . . . I swung the root, heavy with sea water, behind me, and the momentum sped my arm and I gave him, my brother, a blow on the head that forced him to his knees on the sand. . . .

I walked a little way down the beach and turned to watch him, and I was thinking of my own skin then. He had got to his feet and he seemed steady. The daylight was still clear, but on the sea wind fumes of brine were blowing in like a light fog, and when I had walked a little way from him, I <u>could</u> hardly <u>see</u> his dark figure in this obscurity. . . . Then I <u>turned</u> my back on him and as I got near to the house, I <u>went</u> swimming again.

Exercise 8. Literary Discourse Functions

The following passage, from *Native Son,* by Richard Wright, begins in the first paragraph in narrative tense. In the second and third paragraphs, however, a shift takes place from the narrator's voice into the mind of the character, Bigger Thomas. Examine the passage and then identify all of the signals in the discourse indicating that this shift to "free indirect style" has taken place. You should consider especially tense and pronoun in conjunction with adverbials of time and place, demonstratives, or particular forms of questions or exclamations.

Outside his window he saw the sun dying over the rooftops. . . . All day long it had been springlike; but <u>now</u> dark clouds were slowly swallowing the sun. . . .

He went out and walked south to Forty-sixth Street, then eastward. <u>Well</u>, he would see <u>in a few moments</u> if the Daltons for whom he was to work were like the people he had seen and heard in the movie. But while walking through <u>this</u> quiet and spacious white neighborhood, he did not feel the pull and mystery of the thing as strongly as he had in the movie. . . .

<u>Would they expect him to come in the front way or back</u>? . . . Goddamn! He walked the length of the picket fence in front of the house, seeking for a walk leading to the rear. But there was none. . . . <u>Suppose a policeman saw him wandering in a white neighborhood like this</u>? . . .

<u>Aw, what the hell</u>! He had to do better than this. . . . The doorknob turned. The door opened. He saw a white face. It was a woman. . . . "Follow me," she said. With cap in hand and shoulders sloped, he followed. "Take a seat. . . . I'll tell Mr. Dalton that you're here and he'll be out in a moment."

"Yessum."

He sat and looked up at the woman; she was staring at him. . . . He was glad when she left. <u>That old bastard</u>! <u>What's so damn funny</u>?

Exercise 9. Prepositional and Phrasal Verbs

In this passage, from Arthur Miller's play *The Last Yankee,* indicate the type of verb phrase for each underlined structure by writing the corresponding numbers in the blanks following the passage. Use the numbers in the list.

1. Phrasal verb, intransitive
2. Phrasal verb, transitive
3. Prepositional verb
4. Prepositional phrasal verb

Frick: Everybody's got the gimmes. . . . Had a man in a few weeks ago to (1) <u>put in</u> a new shower head. Nothing to it. (2) <u>Screw off</u> the old one and (3) <u>screw on</u> the new one. Seventeen dollars an hour!

Leroy: Everybody's got to live, I guess.

Frick: I (4) <u>take</u> my hat <u>off to</u> you—that kind of independence. . . . What line are you in?

Leroy: Carpenter.

Frick: You say Anthony?

Leroy: No, Hamilton. Leroy.

Frick: Of course! There was a big article about you in the *Herald*. . . . (5) <u>Descended from</u> Alexander Hamilton.

. . .

Frick: Sure! I recognize you. . . . You were out in the yard loading plywood the morning that article (6) <u>came out</u>. . . . What are you fellas charging now?

Leroy: . . . Seventeen an hour.

Frick: Good for you. . . . If they'll pay it, grab it.

1. ___

2. ___

3. ___

4. ___

5. ___

6. ___

Exercise 10. Discourse Functions of Phrasal Verbs

Phrasal verbs are often considered colloquial and can be used to indicate that the discourse is intended as relatively informal. In this passage, from "Salvation," from *The Big Sea,* by Langston Hughes, notice the use of the phrasal verb in the final sentence, "So I *got up.*" Suppose that Hughes had written instead, "So I *arose*" or "So I *rose.*" Comment on any differences you find in terms of the discourse effects, such as whether the impression given is that of a relatively informal narrative, as the informal tone of a young boy. Identify any other differences you see.

With respect to formal or informal tone, comment also on the use of the phrasal verb in lines 1 and 2, "*holding* everything *up* so long" rather than, say, "*delaying* everything so long," and of the use of *maybe* in line 7, "*maybe* to save further trouble," rather than "*perhaps* to save further trouble." Finally, concerning the impression that the narrator is a young boy, comment on any differences you think there might be in this overall impression if the author had instead written *delaying, perhaps,* and *arose* in these instances.

1   Now it was really getting late. I began to be ashamed of myself, holding everything up so long. I began to wonder what God thought about Westley, who certainly hadn't seen Jesus either, but who was now sitting proudly on the platform, swinging his knickerbockered legs and

5   grinning down at me, surrounded by deacons and old women on their knees praying. God had not struck Westley dead for taking his name in vain or for lying in the temple. So I decided that maybe to save further trouble, I'd better lie, too, and say that Jesus had come and get up and be saved.

        So I got up.

Chapter 5
Verb Classes and Sentence Types

Exercise 1. Recognizing Sentence Types

Read the following passage, from Amy Tan's novel *The Kitchen God's Wife*. Considering only the parts in brackets, identify the bracketed structures as one of the seven sentence types by writing the corresponding abbreviations in the blanks following the passage. Use the abbreviations in the list.

SVC	(Subject + verb + complement)
SV	(Subject + verb)
SVO	(Subject + verb + direct object)
SVOO	(Subject + verb + indirect object + direct object)
SVOC	(Subject + verb + direct object + complement)
SVA	(Subject + verb + adverbial)
SVOA	(Subject + verb + direct object + adverbial)

"We better hit the road," says Phil. (1) [I put my teacup down].

"Don't forget," my mother says to Phil. (2) "[Grand Auntie's present is in the laundry room]."

Phil throws me a look of surprise.

"Remember?" I lie. "I told you—what Grand Auntie left us in her will. . . ."

She turns on the light, and then (3) [I see it]. . . . (4) [It is the altar] for Grand Auntie's goodluck god, the Chinese creche.

"And who is this on the inside?" . . .

(5) "Oh, [we call this the Kitchen God]. To my way of thinking, (6) [he is not too important]. Not like Buddha . . . not that high level, not even the same level as the Money God. . . . (7) [He is not Santa Claus.] More like a spy—FBI agent, CIA, Mafia, worse than IRS, that kind of person! (8) [And he does not give *you* gifts], you give *him* things. All year long (9) [you have to show him respect]—give him tea and oranges. When Chinese New Year's time comes, you must give him even better things—maybe whiskey to drink, cigarettes to smoke, candy to eat, that kind of thing. (10) [You are hoping] all the time . . . maybe he reports

good things about you. (11) [This family has been good], you hope he says. (12) [Please give them good luck] next year."

1. _____	7. _____
2. _____	8. _____
3. _____	9. _____
4. _____	10. _____
5. _____	11. _____
6. _____	12. _____

Exercise 2. More on Sentence Types

Read the following passage, from Edith Wharton's story "The Mission of Jane." Considering only the parts in brackets, identify the bracketed structures as one of the seven sentence types by writing the corresponding abbreviations in the blanks following the passage. Use the abbreviations in the list.

SVC   (Subject + verb + complement)
SV   (Subject + verb)
SVO   (Subject + verb + direct object)
SVOO   (Subject + verb + indirect object + direct object)
SVOC   (Subject + verb + direct object + complement)
SVA   (Subject + verb + adverbial)
SVOA   (Subject + verb + direct object + adverbial)

(1) [Most of his wife's opinions were heirlooms], and (2) [he took quaint pleasure] in tracing their descent. (3) [She was proud] of their age, and (4) [(she) saw no reason] for discarding them while (5) [they were still serviceable]. (6) [Some, of course, were so fine] that (7) [she kept them] for state occasions, like her great-grandmother's Crown Derby; but from the lady known as Aunt Sophronia (8) [she had inherited a stout set of everyday prejudices] that were practically as good as new; whereas her husband's, (9) [she noticed], were always having to be replaced. In the early days she had fancied there might be a certain satisfaction in taxing him with the fact; but she had long since been silenced by the reply: "My dear, (10) [I'm not a rich man], but (11) [I never use an opinion twice] if I can help it. . . .

"I'm not in the least ashamed!" she repeated, with the air of shaking a banner to the wind; but the domestic atmosphere being calm, (12) [the banner drooped unheroically].

1. _____	7. _____
2. _____	8. _____
3. _____	9. _____
4. _____	10. _____
5. _____	11. _____
6. _____	12. _____

Exercise 3. Identifying Syntactic Functions

Read the following passage, from Kyoko Mori's story "Yellow Mittens and Early Violets." Identify the underlined phrases according to syntactic function by writing the corresponding abbreviations in the blanks following the passage. Use the abbreviations in the list. (*Hint:* In some cases it may be helpful first to identify the overall sentence pattern, as in exercise 1, and then to decide which functional slot the phrase fills in this particular pattern.)

SC   (Subject complement)   IO   (Indirect object)
OC   (Object complement)   ADV   (Adverbial)
DO   (Direct object)

Masa stepped (1) <u>into the garden</u> in her grey kimono and turned on (2) <u>the light</u>. Her granddaughter Yuki was sitting at the table, putting on and pulling off (3) <u>her yellow mittens</u>. . . .

"Do you want breakfast?"

"No."

Masa went (4) <u>to the sink</u> all the same and measured (5) <u>the rice and water</u> into the saucepan. She filled (6) <u>the tin kettle</u> with fresh water and placed (7) <u>the kettle and the saucepan</u> side by side (8) <u>on the gas stove</u>. Then she struck (9) <u>the match</u> and watched the blue flames appear around the gas rings. The house was (10) <u>heavy</u> with the smell of incense. . . .

Masa sprinkled (11) <u>a small handful of tea leaves</u> (12) <u>into the kettle</u> and sat down opposite Yuki. Yuki continued to read the magazine. It was (13) <u>one of the many</u> she had brought with her on this weekend visit—all of them the kinds of magazines city girls read about make-up, movies, dresses, boys. The yellow mittens lay (14) <u>on the table</u> between Masa and Yuki. They were (15) <u>awkward and crooked</u>, one much larger than the other. Yuki told her that she'd made them herself in a home economics class at the high school.

1. _____	6. _____	11. _____
2. _____	7. _____	12. _____
3. _____	8. _____	13. _____
4. _____	9. _____	14. _____
5. _____	10. _____	15. _____

Exercise 4. Optional and Obligatory Syntactic Functions

Identify the underlined syntactic functions by writing the corresponding abbreviations in the blanks in the first column following the passage. Use the abbreviations in the list. For any indirect objects or adverbials, also identify them as either obligatory or optional by writing OBL or OPT in the blanks in the second column (e.g., in "Jill mailed <u>Jim</u> a letter," the IO is OPT; in "I gave <u>Jim</u> a rose," the IO is OBL). The passage is from Forrest Carter's book *The Education of Little Tree,* Carter's autobiographical remembrances of life with his Eastern Cherokee hill country grandparents.

SC	(Subject complement)	IO	(Indirect object)
OC	(Object complement)	ADV	(Adverbial)
DO	(Direct object)		

In the wintertime, we carried (1) <u>leaves</u> and [we] put (2) <u>them</u> (3) <u>on the corn patch</u>. Back in the hollow, past the barn, the corn patch flattened out (4) <u>on either side of the spring branch</u>. Grandpa had cleared (5) <u>it</u> a little ways up the sides of the mountain. . . . Grandpa called the sloping sides (6) <u>[the "slants],"</u> [which] didn't raise (7) <u>good corn</u>, but he planted (8) <u>it</u> anyhow. There wasn't much flat ground (9) <u>in the hollow</u>.

I liked gathering the leaves and putting them in the two sacks. They were (10) <u>light</u> to carry. Me and Grandpa would carry two, and sometimes three sacks. I tried to carry two, but couldn't make (11) <u>much headway</u> at it. Knee-deep for me, the leaves were like a brown snowfall (12) <u>on the ground</u>, dappled with the yellow paint of maple leaves, and the red of bee gum and sumach bushes.

Function	*OBL/OPT*
1. _____	_____
2. _____	_____
3. _____	_____
4. _____	_____
5. _____	_____
6. _____	_____
7. _____	_____
8. _____	_____
9. _____	_____
10. _____	_____
11. _____	_____
12. _____	_____

Exercise 5. Syntactic Functions of Nouns

For the underlined noun phrases in the following passage, from Toni Morrison's novel *Beloved,* indicate the syntactic functions by writing the corresponding abbreviations in the blanks following the passage. Use the abbreviations in the list.

S (Subject)	SC (Subject complement)	
DO (Direct object)	OC (Object complement)	
IO (Indirect object)		

Beloved is (1) <u>my sister</u>. I swallowed (2) <u>her blood</u> right along with my mother's milk. (3) <u>The first thing</u> I heard . . . was the sound of her crawling up the stairs. She was my secret company until Paul D came. He threw her out. Ever since I was little she was (4) <u>my company</u> and she helped me wait for my daddy. Me and her waited for him. I love (5) <u>my mother</u> but I know she killed one of her own daughters, and tender as she is with me, I'm scared of her because of it. She missed killing my brothers and they knew it. They told (6) <u>me</u> (7) <u>die-witch! stories</u> to show me the way to do it, if ever I needed to. . . . All the time, I'm afraid [that] the thing that happened that made it all right for my mother to kill my sister could happen again. . . . I spent all of my outside self loving Ma'am so she wouldn't kill me, loving her even when she braided my head at night. I never let her know my daddy was coming for me. . . .

My daddy [would] do (8) <u>anything</u> for runny fried eggs. Dip his bread in it. (9) <u>Grandma</u> used to tell me his things. She said anytime she could make (10) <u>him</u> (11) <u>a plate of soft fried eggs</u> [it] was Christmas, [it] made (12) <u>him</u> so happy.

1. _____   7. _____

2. _____   8. _____

3. _____   9. _____

4. _____   10. _____

5. _____   11. _____

6. _____   12. _____

Exercise 6. Syntactic Functions of Adjectives

In the following passage, from Toni Morrison's *Beloved,* repeated from exercise 5, identify the syntactic functions of the underlined adjectives by writing the corresponding abbreviations in the blanks following the passage. Use the abbreviations in the list.

NMOD   (Noun modifier)
SC   (Subject complement)
OC   (Object complement)

Beloved is my sister. I swallowed her blood right along with my mother's milk. The (1) <u>first</u> thing I heard . . . was the sound of her crawling up the stairs. She was my (2) <u>secret</u> company until Paul D came. He threw her out. Ever since I was (3) <u>little</u> she was my company and she helped me wait for my daddy. Me and her waited for him. I love my mother but I know she killed one of her own daughters, and tender as she is with me, I'm scared of her because of it. She missed killing my brothers and they knew it. They told me (4) <u>die-witch!</u> stories to show me the way to do it, if ever I needed to. . . . All the time, I'm (5) <u>afraid</u> [that] the thing that happened that made it all right for my mother to kill my sister could happen again. . . . I spent all of my (6) <u>outside</u> self loving Ma'am so she wouldn't kill me, loving her even when she braided my head at night. I never let her know my daddy was coming for me. . . .

My daddy [would] do anything for (7) <u>runny</u> (8) <u>fried</u> eggs. Dip his bread in it. Grandma used to tell me his things. She said anytime she could make him a plate of (9) <u>soft</u> fried eggs [it] was Christmas, [it] made him so (10) <u>happy</u>.

1. _____	6. _____
2. _____	7. _____
3. _____	8. _____
4. _____	9. _____
5. _____	10. _____

Exercise 7. Semantic Roles and the Narrator's Worldview

Read the following passage, from Liam O'Flaherty's story "The Tent," and answer the questions that follow.

<u>A sudden squall</u> struck <u>the tent</u>. <u>White glittering hailstones</u> struck <u>the shabby canvas</u> with a wild noise. <u>The tent</u> shook and swayed slightly forward, dangling its tattered flaps. <u>The pole</u> creaked as <u>it</u> strained. <u>A rent</u> appeared <u>near the top of the pole</u>. . . . <u>Water</u> immediately trickled <u>through the seam</u>, making a dark blob. <u>A tinker and his two wives</u> were sitting <u>on a heap of straw in the tent</u>, looking out <u>through the entrance at the wild moor</u> that stretched in front of it. . . .

When the squall came <u>the tinker</u> sat up with a start and looked at the pole. <u>He</u> stared at the seam in the canvas, and then <u>he</u> nudged <u>the two women</u> and pointed upwards. . . . <u>The women</u> looked, but nobody spoke. . . . The tinker sighed and struggled to his feet. "<u>I</u>'ll throw <u>a few sacks</u> over the top," he said.

The tinker scrambled up the bank against which the tent was pitched. . . . The force of the squall was so great that <u>it</u> swept <u>through the trees</u> and struck the top of the tent as violently as if it were standing exposed on the open moor. <u>The tinker</u> had to lean against the wind to prevent himself from being carried away. <u>He</u> looked <u>into the wind</u> with wide open nostrils. "It can't last," he said, throwing the two sacks over the tent.

a. Identify the role of each underlined noun phrase in the passage by choosing from the list. Write the role beneath the line where the noun phrase appears.

Agent	Source
Patient	Goal
Instrument	Path
Experiencer	Location
Force	Possessor

b. Throughout the passage, what is/are the dominant role(s) of the subject noun phrases?

c. How would the role relationships change if the tinker and his wives had "seen" the wild moor rather than "looking at" it (paragraph 1) and if the tinker had "noticed" the seam in the canvas rather than "staring" at it (paragraph 2)?

d. What conclusions do you draw about the relationship between the nomadic tinker and his wives and about the violent forces of nature?

Exercise 8. Semantic Roles and the Character's Worldview

Semantic roles are also used at times to express a view of the world that is the character's view and not that of a narrator. An example is the worldview of Lok, a Neanderthal man in William Golding's *The Inheritors,* discussed in an early analysis of subject and verb relations by M. A. K. Halliday. Halliday notes that, in the world that Lok observes, people act but they do not act on things; they move but they move only themselves, not other objects. Further, a high proportion of the subjects is not people but is either parts of the body or inanimate objects, and there appear to be no cause and effect. It is, Halliday says, as if doing is as passive as seeing and things are no more affected by actions than by perceptions.

Read the passage and answer the questions that follow. (*Note:* The stick that grows shorter and then shoots out to full length again is a bow being used to shoot an arrow at Lok.)

The bushes twitched again. Lok steadied himself by the tree and gazed. A head and a chest faced him, half hidden. . . . The man turned side-ways in the bushes and looked at Lok along his shoulder. A stick rose upright and there was a lump of bone in the middle. Lok peered at the stick. . . . Suddenly Lok understood that the man was holding the stick out to him but neither he nor Lok could reach across the river. The stick began to grow shorter at both ends. Then it shot out to full length again.

The dead tree by Lok's ear acquired a voice.

"Clop!"

His ears twitched and he turned to the tree. By his face there had grown a twig. . . . This twig had a white bone at the end. There were hooks in the bone and sticky brown stuff hung in the crooks. His nose examined this stuff and did not like it. He smelled along the shaft of the twig. The leaves on the twig were red feathers and reminded him of goose. He was lost in a generalized astonishment and excitement.

a. Identify the role of each underlined noun phrase, based on what Lok's worldview appears to be; write the role beneath the line in which the noun phrase appears.

Agent	Source
Patient	Goal
Instrument	Path
Experiencer	Location
Force	Possessor

b. Discuss these roles and the extent to which you think they are involved in the discourse effects described by Halliday (as outlined in the first paragraph of this exercise).

Chapter 6
Pronouns, Pro-forms, and Ellipsis

Exercise 1. Identifying Antecedents

In the following passage, from William Golding's essay "Thinking as a Hobby," identify the antecedent for each underlined word or phrase and write it in the corresponding blank following the passage.

While (1) <u>I</u> was still a boy, I came to the conclusion that there were three grades of thinking; and since I was later to claim thinking as (2) <u>my</u> hobby, I came to an even stranger conclusion—namely, that I (3) <u>myself</u> could not think at all.

I must have been an unsatisfactory child for grownups to deal with. I remember how incomprehensible (4) <u>they</u> appeared at first, but not, of course, how I appeared to (5) <u>them</u>. It was the headmaster of my grammar school who first brought the subject of thinking before (6) <u>me</u>. . . . He had some statuettes in (7) <u>his</u> study. . . . One was a lady wearing nothing but a bath towel. (8) <u>She</u> seemed frozen in an eternal panic lest the bath towel slip down any farther; and since she had no arms, she was in an unfortunate position to pull (9) <u>the towel</u> up again. Next to (10) <u>her</u> crouched a leopard. . . . Beyond (11) <u>the leopard</u> was a naked, muscular gentleman, who sat, looking down, with (12) <u>his</u> chin on his fist and his elbow on his knee. He seemed utterly miserable.

Some time later, I learned about (13) <u>these statuettes</u>. The headmaster had placed (14) <u>them</u> where they would face delinquent children, because they symbolized to (15) <u>him</u> the whole of life. . . . It is easy to buy small plaster models of what you think life is like.

1. _deictic_
2. _deictic_
3. _deictic_
4. _anaphor_ — *refers back to grownups*
5. _anaphor_
6. _deictic_
7. _anaphor — refers to lady_
8. _anaphor_
9. _anaphor — pro-form_
10. _anaphor — refers to lady_

(Info = missing) 11. anaphor - proform   14. anaphor
12. anaphor refers to gent 15. anaphor
13. anaphor - proform

Exercise 2. Distinguishing Pronouns and Pro-forms

Identify the underlined forms as either personal, possessive, or reflexive pronouns (the central pronouns) or as pro-forms by writing the corresponding numbers in the blanks following the passage. Use the numbers in the list. For reference, see sections 6.2 and 6.4 of chapter 6 in the textbook. The passage is from the novel *The Piano,* by Jane Campion and Kate Pullinger. Ada, with her small daughter, Flora, has just arrived in a strange land to meet her new husband for the first time. Her belongings, including her piano, sit on the beach waiting to be transported to her new home.

1. Personal pronoun
2. Possessive pronoun
3. Reflexive pronoun
4. Pro-form

Stewart turned away without comment, as though Flora had not spoken. (1) He strode across the sand. . . . "Baines, tell them to carry in pairs. . . ." He waved one hand dismissively at the baggage. . . .

"What do you think?" Stewart kept (2) his voice low, nodding toward Ada.

(3) "She looks tired," [Baines] said eventually.

"She's stunted, (4) that's one thing," Stewart answered abruptly. . . .

Ada opened (5) her notepad again and wrote upon (6) it. Flora carried the white slip of paper to Stewart. "The piano?" the note read.

"Oh no, (7) it can't come now," Stewart said decisively.

"It must," affirmed Flora. (8) "She wants it to come."

"Yes, and (9) so do I," he spoke plainly to the child as (10) they walked back to where Ada and the piano stood. "But there are too few of (11) us here to carry it now," he explained. . . .

Ada signed to Flora, who translated, (12) "We can't leave the piano."

"Let's not discuss (13) this any further. I'm very pleased that you've arrived safely. . . ."

She gripped Flora's hand, anchoring (14) herself to the only thing she had left in the world. (15) <u>She</u> would return, she told herself, she would find a way to retrieve the piano from the beach.

1. __	9. __
2. __	10. __
3. __	11. __
4. __	12. __
5. __	13. __
6. __	14. __
7. __	15. __
8. __	

Exercise 3. Recognizing Ellipted Structures

Identify the material that has been ellipted from the underlined "gaps" in the sentences in this passage, from Sandra Cisneros's novel *The House on Mango Street,* by writing the ellipted material in the corresponding blanks following the passage. Follow the example.

> *Example:* I'd like to read that note, if I may (1) _____.
>   (1) <u>read that note</u>

It wasn't as if I didn't want to work. I did (1) _____. . . . I needed money. The Catholic high school cost a lot. . . .

And though I hadn't started looking yet, I thought I might (2) __ _____ the week after next. But when I came home that afternoon, all wet because Tito had pushed me into the open water hydrant—only I had sort of let him (3) _____—Mama called me in the kitchen before I could even go and change, and Aunt Lala was sitting there. . . . She had found a job for me at the Peter Pan Photo Finishers. . . .

It was real easy . . . except you got tired . . . , and then I started sitting down only when the two ladies next to me did (4) _____. After a while they started to laugh and came up to me and said I could sit when I wanted to (5) _____, and I said I knew (6) _____.

1. _____

2. _____

3. _____

4. _____

5. _____

6. _____

Exercise 4. Distinguishing Categories of Pronominals

For the underlined pronominals in this passage, from *My Antonia* by Willa Cather, indicate their category by writing the corresponding numbers in the blanks following the passage. Use the numbers in the list. (*Note:* Not all categories in the list appear in the passage.)

1. Personal pronoun
2. Possessive pronoun
3. Reflexive pronoun
4. Demonstrative pronoun
5. Indefinite pronoun
6. Interrogative pronoun
7. Pro-form
8. Ellipsis

On the morning of the twenty-second (1) I wakened with a start. Before I opened (2) my eyes, I seemed to know that something had happened. I heard excited voices in the kitchen—(3) grandmother's was so shrill that I knew she must be beside (4) herself. I looked forward to any new crisis with delight. What could (5) it be, I wondered, as I hurried into my clothes.

Down in the kitchen grandfather was standing before the stove with (6) his hands behind (7) him. Jake and Otto had taken off (8) their boots and were rubbing their woolen socks. Grandmother motioned (9) me to the dining-room. Her lips were tightly compressed and she kept whispering to herself: "Oh dear Saviour! (10) Thou knowest!"

Presently grandfather came in and spoke to me: "Jimmy, (11) we will not have prayers this morning, because we have a great deal to do. Old Mr. Shimerda is dead, and his family are in great distress. Ambrosch came over here in the middle of the night, and Jake and Otto went back with him. (12) <u>That</u> is Ambrosch, asleep on the bench.

"No, sir," Fuchs said in answer to a question from grandfather, (13) "<u>nobody</u> heard the gun go off."

"Poor soul, poor soul!" grandmother groaned. "I'd like to think he never done (14) <u>it</u>. How could he forget himself and bring (15) <u>this</u> on us!"

1. ___	6. ___	11. ___
2. ___	7. ___	12. ___
3. ___	8. ___	13. ___
4. ___	9. ___	14. ___
5. ___	10. ___	15. ___

Exercise 5. Anaphora and Deixis

Read the following passage, from R. K. Narayan's story "A Horse and Two Goats." Decide which of the underlined pronominals are anaphoric (A) and which are deictic (D) and write the corresponding letters in the blanks following the passage.

The stranger almost pinioned Muni's back to the statue and asked, "Isn't this statue (1) <u>yours</u>? Why don't you sell (2) <u>it</u> to (3) <u>me</u>?"

(4) <u>The old man</u> now understood the reference to the horse, thought for a second, and said in (5) <u>his</u> own language, "(6) <u>I</u> was an urchin this high when I heard my grandfather explain this horse and warrior, and my grandfather (7) <u>himself</u> was this high when he heard (8) <u>his</u> grandfather, (9) <u>whose</u> grandfather. . . ."

(10) <u>The other man</u> interrupted him with, "(11) <u>I</u> don't want to seem to have stopped here for nothing. I will offer (12) <u>you</u> a good price for (13) <u>this</u>," he said, indicating the horse. (14) <u>He</u> had concluded that Muni owned this mud horse. . . . (15) "<u>You</u> don't have to waste your breath in sales talk. I appreciate the article. You don't have to explain (16) <u>its</u> points."

"I never went to school, in those days only Brahmin went to schools, but (17) <u>we</u> had to . . . work in the fields morning till night . . . and when Pongal came and we had cut the harvest, (18) <u>my</u> father allowed me to go out and play with others at the tank, and so I don't know the Parangi language you speak. . . . We had a postman in our village (19) <u>who</u> could speak to you boldly in your language, but (20) <u>his</u> wife ran away with someone and he does not speak to anyone at all nowadays."

1. __	6. __	11. __	16. __
2. __	7. __	12. __	17. __
3. __	8. __	13. __	18. __
4. __	9. __	14. __	19. __
5. __	10. __	15. __	20. __

Exercise 6. Discourse Functions

Read the following passage, noting the discourse functions of the underlined pronouns. Rewrite the passage, changing the underlined pronouns back into their antecedent phrases. Then write a paragraph commenting on the functions and effects of pronouns in discourse. The passage is from the opening paragraphs of "Flowering Judas," a short story by Katherine Anne Porter.

> Braggioni sits heaped upon the edge of a straight-backed chair much too small for him, and sings to Laura in a furry, mournful voice. Laura has begun to find reasons for avoiding her own house until the latest possible moment, for Braggioni is there almost every night. No matter how late <u>she</u> is, <u>he</u> will be sitting there with a surly, waiting expression, pulling at his kinky hair, thumbing the strings of his guitar, snarling a tune under his breath.
>
> Laura wishes to lie down, <u>she</u> is tired of her hairpins and the feel of her long tight sleeves, but <u>she</u> says to <u>him</u>, "Have you a new song for me this evening?" If <u>he</u> says yes, <u>she</u> asks <u>him</u> to sing it. If <u>he</u> says no, <u>she</u> remembers his favorite one, and asks <u>him</u> to sing it again. Lupe brings <u>her</u> a cup of chocolate and a plate of rice, and Laura eats at the small table under the lamp, first inviting Braggioni, whose answer is always the same, "I have eaten, and besides, chocolate thickens the voice."

Exercise 7. Pronouns and Discourse Functions in Narrative

Read the following passage, paying attention to the effects created by the use of pronouns. Then write a paragraph commenting on the point of view the author seems to be establishing and on how the use of pronouns contributes to that point of view. (See also chap. 2 of the textbook for discussion of "point of view" in narrative.) The passage is from the opening paragraphs of Ring Lardner's story "Who Dealt?"

You know, this is the first time Tom and I have been with real friends since we were married. I suppose you'll think it's funny for me to call you *my* friends when we've never met before, but Tom has talked about you so much and how much he thought of you and how crazy he was to see you and everything. . . .

Arthur and Helen, Arthur and Helen—he talks about you so much that it's a wonder I'm not jealous; especially of you, Helen. You must have been his real pal when you were kids.

No, thank you, Arthur; no more. Two is my limit and I've already exceeded it, with two cocktails before dinner and now this. But it's a special occasion, meeting Tom's best friends. I bet Tom wishes he could celebrate too, don't you, dear? . . . He's got the strongest will-power of any person I ever saw.

I do think it's wonderful, him staying on the wagon this long, a man that used—well, you know as well as I do; probably a whole lot better, because you were with him so much in the old days, and all I know is just what he's told me. He told me about once in Pittsburgh—All right, Tommie; I won't say another word. But it's all over now, thank heavens! Not a drop since we've been married: three whole months! And he says it's forever, don't you dear?

Chapter 7

Prepositions and Prepositional Phrases

Exercise 1. Formal Aspects of Prepositional Constructions

In chapter 3 of this workbook you were asked to identify adjectives and adverbs in Robert Frost's poem "A Considerable Speck." Now consider the prepositional constructions in the following excerpt from Frost's poem and indicate the type of structure by writing the corresponding numbers in the blank, following the poem. Use the numbers in the list. (*Note:* Some of the structures in the list may not appear in this excerpt.)

1. Preposition + noun phrase complement	(Prepositional phrase)
2. Preposition + V-*ing* complement	(Prepositional phrase)
3. Preposition + *wh-* clause complement	(Prepositional phrase)
4. Complex preposition	(Adverb or preposition + preposition)
5. Directional adverb	(Ordinary adverb)
6. Ellipted prepositional phrase as directional adverb	("Bare" preposition)
7. Prepositional verb	(Verb + preposition)
8. Phrasal verb	(Verb + adverbial particle)

A speck that would have been (1) [beneath my sight]
(2) [On any but a paper sheet so white]
(3) [Set off] (4) [across what I had written there].
And I had idly poised my pen (5) [in air]
To stop it with a period (6) [of ink]
When something strange about it made me think.
This was no dust speck (7) [by my breathing] blown,
But unmistakably a living mite
(8) [With inclinations] it could call its own.
It paused as (9) [with suspicion] (10) [of my pen],
And then came wildly racing (11) [on] again

(12) [To where my manuscript was not yet dry];
Then paused again and either drank or smelt—
(13) [With loathing], for again it turned to fly.
Plainly with an intelligence I dealt.
It seemed too tiny to have room (14) [for feet],
Yet must have had a set (15) [of them] complete
To express how much it didn't want to die.

1. __   6. __   11. __

2. __   7. __   12. __

3. __   8. __   13. __

4. __   9. __   14. __

5. __   10. __   15. __

Exercise 2. More Practice with Formal Aspects

As in exercise 1, indicate the type of structure by writing the corresponding numbers in the blanks following the passage. Use the numbers in the list. This passage is from the opening paragraphs of William Faulkner's novel *The Sound and the Fury.*

1. Preposition + noun phrase complement   (Prepositional phrase)
2. Preposition + V-*ing* complement   (Prepositional phrase)
3. Preposition + *wh-* clause complement   (Prepositional phrase)
4. Complex preposition   (Adverb or preposition + preposition)
5. Directional adverb   (Ordinary adverb)
6. Ellipted prepositional phrase as directional adverb   ("Bare" preposition)
7. Prepositional verb   (Verb + preposition)
8. Phrasal verb   (Verb + adverbial particle)

(1) [Through the fence], (2) [between the curling flower spaces], I could see them hitting. They were coming (3) [toward where the flag was], and I went (4) [along the fence]. Luster was hunting (5) [in the grass] (6) [by the flower tree]. They took the flag (7) [out], and they were hitting. They put the flag (8) [back], and they went (9) [to the table], and he hit and the other hit. Then they went (10) [on], and I went along the fence. Luster came (11) [away from the flower tree] and we went

along the fence and they stopped and we stopped and (12) [looked through the fence] while Luster was hunting (13) [in the grass].

"Here, caddie." He hit. They went (14) [away across the pasture]. I held (15) [to the fence] and watched them going (16) [away].

"(17) [Listen at you,] now," Luster said. "Aint you something, thirty-three years old, (18) [going on] that way. After I done went all the way (19) [to town] to buy you that cake. Hush up that moaning. Aint you going to help me find that quarter so I can go (20) [to the show] tonight."

1. ___   6. ___   11. ___   16. ___

2. ___   7. ___   12. ___   17. ___

3. ___   8. ___   13. ___   18. ___

4. ___   9. ___   14. ___   19. ___

5. ___   10. ___   15. ___   20. ___

Exercise 3. Functions of Prepositional Phrases

Consider again the excerpt from Robert Frost's poem "A Considerable Speck," repeated from exercise 1. Indicate the functions of the bracketed phrases (or words) by writing them in the blanks following the passage, choosing from the lists given. (*Note:* Some categories may not appear in this passage.)

Adverbials   *Complements*
Location   Noun complement (NC)
Goal   Adjective complement (ADJC)
Source   Verb complement (VC)
Path
Time
Manner
Instrument
Accompaniment

> A speck that would have been (1) [beneath my sight]
> (2) [On any but a paper sheet so white]
> Set off (3) [across what I had written there].
> And I had idly poised my pen (4) [in air]
> To stop it (5) [with a period] (6) [of ink]
> When something strange (7) [about it] made me think.

This was no dust speck (8) [by my breathing blown],
But unmistakably a living mite
(9) [With inclinations] it could call its own.
It paused as (10) [with suspicion] (11) [of my pen],
And then came wildly racing on again
(12) [To where my manuscript was not yet dry];
Then paused again and either drank or smelt—
(13) [With loathing], for again it turned to fly.
Plainly with an intelligence I dealt.
It seemed too tiny to have room (14) [for feet],
Yet must have had a set (15) [of them] complete
To express how much it didn't want to die.

1. _____   6. _____   11. _____

2. _____   7. _____   12. _____

3. _____   8. _____   13. _____

4. _____   9. _____   14. _____

5. _____   10. _____   15. _____

Exercise 4. More Practice with Functions of Prepositional Phrases

In this passage from William Faulkner's novel *The Sound and the Fury*, repeated from exercise 2, indicate the functions of the bracketed phrases (or words) by writing them in the blanks following the passage, choosing from the list. (*Note:* Some categories may not appear in this passage.)

Adverbials	*Complements*
Location	Noun complement (NC)
Goal	Adjective complement (ADJC)
Source	Verb complement (VC)
Path	
Time	
Manner	
Instrument	
Accompaniment	

(1) [Through the fence], (2) [between the curling flower spaces], I could see them hitting. They were coming (3) [toward where the flag

was], and I went (4) [along the fence]. Luster was hunting (5) [in the grass] (6) [by the flower tree]. They took the flag out, and they were hitting. They put the flag back, and they went (7) [to the table], and he hit and the other hit. Then they went on, and I went along the fence. Luster came (8) [away from the flower tree] and we went along the fence and they stopped and we stopped and (9) [looked through the fence] while Luster was hunting in the grass.

"Here, caddie." He hit. They went (10) [away across the pasture]. I held to the fence and watched them going away.

"Listen at you, now," Luster said. "Aint you something, thirty-three years old, going on that way. After I done went all the way (11) [to town] to buy you that cake. Hush up that moaning. Aint you going to help me find that quarter so I can go (12) [to the show] tonight."

1. _____
2. _____
3. _____
4. _____
5. _____
6. _____

7. _____
8. _____
9. _____
10. _____
11. _____
12. _____

Exercise 5. Discourse Functions: Prepositional Phrases and Spatial Relations

As you read the opening passage from Joseph Conrad's novel *The Secret Sharer,* pay special attention to the spatial relations indicated by the prepositional phrases. Comment on the role of the underlined prepositional phrases in expressing various spatial relationships among parts of the discourse, in particular the role of these phrases in helping to create a detailed scene, as we envision it, in relation to the vantage point of the narrator (see chap. 7, in the textbook, section 7.2).

1   On my right hand there were lines of fishing-stakes resembling a mysterious system of half-submerged bamboo fences, incomprehensible in its division of the domain of tropical fishes, and crazy of aspect as if abandoned forever by some nomad tribe of fishermen now gone to the other
5   end of the ocean; for there was no sign of human habitation as far as the eye could reach. To the left a group of barren islets, suggesting ruins of stone walls, towers, and blockhouses, had its foundations set in a blue

sea that itself looked solid, so still and stable did it lie <u>below my feet</u>;
even the track of light from the westering sun shone smoothly, without

10 that animated glitter which tells of an imperceptible ripple. And when
I turned my head to take a parting glance at the tug which had just left
us anchored <u>outside the bar</u>, I saw the straight line of the flat shore joined
<u>to the stable sea</u>, edge <u>to edge</u>, with a perfect and unmarked closeness,
in one levelled floor half brown, half blue <u>under the enormous dome</u>

15 <u>of the sky</u>.

Exercise 6. Discourse Functions: Prepositional Phrases and Temporal Relations

In chapter 4, exercise 7, you were asked to read a passage from John Cheever's
story "Goodbye, My Brother" and to note the chronological order of events as
expressed by the underlined tense and aspect forms and their sequencing. Review your answers to exercise 7 and then reread the portion of the passage repeated here, noting this time the discourse role of prepositional phrases and the
way in which they contribute to the coherence of the passage with respect to
temporal relations.

Comment especially about the complementary role of prepositional phrases
and tense and aspect forms in helping the reader keep track of temporal relations
among the various events as they are recalled by the narrator. (Tense and aspect
forms are underlined; prepositional phrases of time are enclosed in brackets.)

"I don't like it here," Lawrence <u>said</u> bluntly, without raising his eyes. "I'm
going to sell my equity in the house to Chaddy. . . . The only reason I
came back was to say goodbye."

I <u>let</u> him get ahead and I <u>walked</u> behind him, looking at his shoulders and thinking of all the goodbyes he <u>had made</u>. When Father
<u>drowned</u>, he <u>went</u> to the church and <u>said</u> goodbye to Father. It was only
three years later that he <u>concluded</u> that Mother was frivolous and <u>said</u>
goodbye to her. [In his freshman year] at college, he <u>had been</u> good
friends with his roommate, but the man <u>drank</u> too much, and [at the
beginning of the spring term] Lawrence <u>changed</u> roommates and <u>said</u>
goodbye to his friend. When he <u>had been</u> in college [for two years], he
<u>concluded</u> that the atmosphere was too sequestered and he <u>said</u> good-
bye to Yale. He <u>enrolled</u> at Columbia and <u>got</u> his law degree there, but
he <u>found</u> his first employer dishonest, and [at the end of six months] he
<u>said</u> goodbye to a good job. He <u>married</u> Ruth in City Hall and <u>said</u>
goodbye to the Protestant Episcopal Church; they <u>went</u> to live on a back
street in Tuckahoe and <u>said</u> goodbye to the middle class.

Exercise 7. Discourse Functions: Narrator's Point of View

In the opening passage from William Faulkner's novel *The Sound and the Fury*, repeated from exercise 2, the point of view is that of an adult man, Benji, who is severely mentally disabled. Discuss the role of the underlined prepositional phrases of place in creating the somewhat disjointed description we get of the golf course and of the people playing golf, as seen through Benji's eyes. Consider especially how these phrases help to create a scene that is slightly bewildering, which in turn contributes to the growing impression that the mental state of the narrator is somehow abnormal.

> (1) Through the fence, (2) between the curling flower spaces, I could see them hitting. They were coming (3) toward where the flag was, and I went (4) along the fence. Luster was hunting (5) in the grass (6) by the flower tree. They took the flag out, and they were hitting. They put the flag back, and they went (7) to the table, and he hit and the other hit. Then they went on, and I went (8) along the fence. Luster came (9) away from the flower tree and we went (10) along the fence and they stopped and we stopped and (11) looked through the fence while Luster was hunting in the grass.
>
> "Here, caddie." He hit. They went (12) away across the pasture. I held to the fence and watched them going away.

Exercise 8. Functions of Complex Prepositional Phrases

Several complex prepositional phrases appear in the following passage, from Cormac McCarthy's novel *Suttree*. Discuss whether they are "single" function phrases that add more emphasis or are "dual" function phrases that create additional adverbial meaning (see chap. 7 in the textbook, sections 7.3.2 and 7.3.3).

> Joe was watching him. Listen, he said. You could get on (1) up at Miller's (on the hill). Brother said they needed somebody in Men's Shoes.
>
> Suttree looked at the ground and smiled and wiped his mouth with the back of his wrist and looked up again. Well, he said, I guess I'll just stick to the river for a while yet.
>
> They lifted each a hand in farewell and he watched the boy go (2) up on the tracks and then across the fields toward the road. Then he went (3) down to the skiff and pulled the rope up and tossed it in and pushed off into the river again. The dead man was still lying on the bank under his blanket but the crowd had begun to drift away. He rowed (4) on across the river. He swung the skiff (5) in beneath the bridge and sat looking down at the fish.

Chapter 8

Coordinate Structures
and Complex Sentences

Exercise 1. Recognizing Coordinate Structures

For the conjoined structures in the following passage, the second coordinate in a pair (or the third in a series) is enclosed in brackets. Identify each according to the type of structure that is coordinated and write the corresponding numbers in the blanks following the passage. Use the numbers in the list. The passage is from an essay by James Carroll, "An American Requiem."

1. Clause – SV
2. Verb phrase
3. Noun phrase
4. Adjective phrase
5. Adverb phrase
6. Prepositional phrase

My father: not until years later did I appreciate how commanding was his presence. As a boy, I was aware of the admiring glances he drew as he walked into the Officers' Club, (1) [but I thought nothing of them]. I used to see him in the corridors of the Pentagon, where I would go after school (2) [and then ride home with him]. I sensed the regard people had for him, (3) [but I assumed that his warmth (4) [and goodness] were common to everyone of his rank]. I had no way of knowing how unlikely was the story of his success, (5) [nor had I any way to grasp the difference between him and other Air Force generals]. He was as tall as they, (6) [but looked more like a movie actor]. I saw him stand at banquet tables as the speaker at communion breakfast, at sports-team dinners, (7) [and, once, at a German-American Friendship Gala in Berlin]. His voice was resonant (8) [and firm]. He approved of laughter (9) [and could evoke it easily], though he never told jokes. His mode of public speaking had a touch of the preacher in it. He brought fervor to what he said, (10) [and a display of one naked feeling: an unrestrained love of his country].

goodness = noun

1. _1_   3. _1_   5. _1_   7. _6_   9. _2_
2. _2_   4. _3_   6. _2_   8. _4_   10. _3_

61

Exercise 2. Recognizing Adverbial and Nominal Clauses

For the clauses enclosed in brackets in the following passage, identify each according to type and write the corresponding numbers in the blanks following the passage. Use the numbers in the list. The excerpt given is from the final scene of Henry James's novella *Daisy Miller,* when Winterbourne discovers that Daisy is ill. (*Note:* In some cases there may be embedded clauses within other embedded clauses, indicated [( )].)

1. Adverbial clause
2. Nominal *that* clause
3. Nominal *wh-* clause
4. Nominal infinitive clause
5. Nominal gerundive clause

    Winterbourne, (1) [when the rumour came to him], immediately went to the hotel for more news. He found (2) [that two or three charitable friends had preceded him], and that they were being entertained in Mrs. Miller's salon by Randolph.

    "It's going round at night," said Randolph—"that's (3) [what made her sick]. She likes (4) [going round at night]. I shouldn't think (5) [she'd want to]—it's so plaguy dark." Mrs. Miller was invisible; she was now, at least, giving her daughter the advantage of her society. It was evident that Daisy was dangerously ill. . . .

    "Daisy spoke of you the other day," Mrs. Miller said to him. "Half the time she doesn't know (6) [what she's saying], but that time I think (7) [she did]. She gave me a message; she told me to tell you that she was never engaged to that handsome Italian. I'm sure I am very glad; Mr. Giovanelli hasn't been near us (8) [since she was taken ill]. I thought (9) [he was so much of a gentleman]; but I don't call that very polite! Anyway, she says (10) [she's not engaged]. I don't know (11) [why she wanted (12) (you to know)]; but she said to me three times, 'Mind you tell Mr. Winterbourne.' And then she told me to ask (13) [if you remembered the time you went to that castle in Switzerland]. But I said (14) [I wouldn't give any such messages as that]. Only, (15) [if she is not engaged], I'm sure glad to know it."

1. ___	6. ___	11. ___
2. ___	7. ___	12. ___
3. ___	8. ___	13. ___
4. ___	9. ___	14. ___
5. ___	10. ___	15. ___

Exercise 3. Distinguishing Adverbial Clause Functions

Indicate the functions of the adverbial clauses in brackets by writing the corresponding functions in the blanks following the passage. Use the items in the list. The passage is from Mark Twain's article about his experiences as an apprentice pilot on a steamboat, "Old Times on the Mississippi."

Adverbial Clause Functions

Time	Reason
Place	Cause
Condition	Purpose
Concession	Manner
Result	

During the afternoon watch the next day, Mr. Bixby asked me if I knew how to run the next few miles. I said:

"Go inside the first snag above the point, outside the next one, start out from the lower end of Higgin's woodyard, make a square crossing, and—"

"That's all right. I'll be back (1) [before you close up on the next point]."

But he wasn't. He was still below (2) [when I rounded it and entered upon a piece of river which I had some misgivings about]. I did not know that he was hiding behind a chimney (3) [to see how I would perform]. I went gaily along, getting prouder and prouder, (4) [because he had never left the boat in my sole charge such a length of time before]. I even got to "setting" her and letting the wheel go entirely (5) [while I vaingloriously turned my back and inspected the stern marks and hummed a tune], a sort of easy indifference which I had prodigiously admired in Bixby and other pilots. Once I inspected rather long, and (6) [when I faced to the front again] my heart flew into my mouth (7) [so suddenly that I should have lost it] (8) [if I hadn't clapped my teeth together]. One of those frightful bluff reefs was stretching its deadly length right across our bows! My head was gone in a minute; I did not know which end I stood on; I gasped and could not get my breath; I spun the wheel down with (9) [such rapidity that it wove itself together like a spider's web]; the boat answered and turned square away from the reef, but the reef followed her! I fled, but still it followed, still it kept—right across my bows! I never looked to see where I was going, I only fled. The awful crash was imminent. Why didn't that villain come? (10) [If I committed the crime of ringing a bell] I might get thrown overboard. But better that than kill the boat. So in blind desperation, I started (11) [such a rattling "shivaree" down below that the engineers must have been astounded]. Amidst the frenzy of the bells the engines began to back and fill in a curious way, and my reason forsook its throne—we were about to crash into the woods on the other side of the river. Just then Mr. Bixby stepped calmly into view on the hurricane-deck. He blandly and sweetly took his toothpick out of his mouth between his fingers, (12) [as if it were a cigar]—we were just in the act of climbing an overhanging big tree, and the passengers were scudding astern like rats—and lifted up these commands to me ever so gently:

"Stop the larboard! Come ahead on it! Stop the starboard! Come ahead on it! Point her for the bar!"

I sailed away as serenely as a summer's morning. Mr. Bixby came in and said, with mock simplicity: (13) "[When you have a hail], my boy, you ought to tap the big bell three times (14) [before you land], (15) [so that the engineers can get ready]."

1. _____   6. _____   11. _____

2. _____   7. _____   12. _____

3. _____   8. _____   13. _____

4. _____   9. _____   14. _____

5. _____   10. _____   15. _____

Exercise 4. Distinguishing Subordinate Adverbials and Sentence Adverbials

In the following passage, from the novel *Wide Sargasso Sea,* by Jean Rhys, indicate whether each underlined adverb is a subordinator in a subordinate adverbial clause or a sentence adverbial in a main clause by writing the appropriate abbreviations in the blanks following the passage. Use the abbreviations in the list.

SUB ADV   (Adverbial subordinator)
SENT ADV   (Sentence adverbial)

I don't how long it was (1) [before I began to feel chilly. . . .] I had better get back before dark, I thought. The light had changed and the shadows were long. Then I saw a little girl carrying a large basket on her head. I met her eyes and to my astonishment she screamed loudly. . . .

(2) [Then she disappeared]. I must be within a few minutes of the path I thought, but (3) [after I had walked for what seemed a long time] I found that . . . the trees closed over my head. . . . I was lost and afraid among these enemy trees, so certain of danger that (4) [when I heard footsteps and a shout] I did not answer. . . .

I did not look up (5) [though I saw him at the window] but rode on without thinking (6) [till I came to the rocks]. People here call them Mounes Mors (the Dead Ones). Preston shied at them; they say horses always do. (7) [Then he stumbled badly], so I dismounted and walked . . . to Christophine's two-roomed house. . . . I had seen her so often standing knee deep in the river. . . . (8) [Sometimes there would be other women all bringing their washing down on the stones again and again]. . . . The sky was dark blue through the dark green mango leaves, and I thought, "This is my place and this is where I belong."

1. _____   5. _____

2. _____   6. _____

3. _____   7. _____

4. _____   8. _____

Exercise 5. Distinguishing Nominal Functions

For the nominal clauses in brackets, distinguish each according to its grammatical function by writing subject (S), object (O), or subject complement (SC) in the preceding blank. The passage is again from Henry James's novel *Daisy Miller,* early in the story when Winterbourne is first being introduced. (*Note:* For blanks (5)–(7) the structure involves an embedding within an embedding—blanks (5) and (6) refer to the functions of the two clauses [enclosed in parentheses] in relation to the verb *was;* blank (7) [placed at the <u>end</u> of the sentence] refers to the function of the entire structure within the curly brackets "{ }," in relation to the preceding verb *affirmed.*)

I hardly know (1) _____ [whether it was the analogies or the differences that were uppermost in the mind of a young American], who, two or three years ago, sat in the garden of the "Trois Couronnes." He was some seven-and-twenty years of age; when his friends spoke of him, they usually said (2) _____ [that he was at Geneva], "studying." He was an extremely amiable fellow, and universally liked. (3) _____ [What I should say] is, simply (4) _____ [that when certain persons spoke of him] they affirmed {(5) _____ (that the reason of his spending so much time at Geneva) was (6) _____ (that he was extremely devoted to a lady who lived there) (7) _____ }.

He had now finished his breakfast, but he was drinking a small cup of coffee.

Winterbourne looked along the path and saw a beautiful young lady advancing. "American girls are the best girls," he said cheerfully to his young companion.

He wondered (8) _____ [whether he had gone too far]; but he decided (9) _____ [that he must advance farther], rather than retreat. While he was thinking of something else to say, the young lady turned to the little boy.

"I should like (10) _____ [to know (11) _____ (where you got that pole)]," she said.

He asked (12) _____ [if she should not be more comfortable in sitting upon the bench which he had just quitted]. She answered (13) _____ [that she liked (14) _____ (standing up and walking about)]; but she presently sat down. She said (15) _____ [she was from New York].

Exercise 6. Coordinate Structures and Internal Modification

In the paragraph in version A, from Annie Dillard's *Pilgrim at Tinker's Creek,* there are two coordinate sentences numbered as (1) and (2). Both contain internal modification, in each case a prepositional phrase beginning with *like.* In the rewritten version in B, the underlined modifiers appear instead in separate sentences. Discuss these two versions, comparing them in terms of the following.

(a) The relative smoothness or choppiness of the paragraph
(b) The overall coherence
(c) Any differences you see concerning the special emphasis or "end focus" given to the sudden discovery of *the praying mantis* by means of its sentence final position. (Note especially the expanded coordinate sentence in version A as compared with the independent sentences that intervene between the first and second coordinates *I saw X . . . and then I saw Y* in version B, i.e., *Y = the praying mantis*.) (See also chaps. 1 and 11 in the textbook for discussion of end focus.)

Version A
I had been ambling across this hill for several hours that day, when suddenly I noticed a speck of pure white. . . . (1) I leaned to examine the white thing and [I] saw a mass of bubbles <u>like spittle</u>. (2) Then I saw something dark <u>like an engorged leech</u> rummaging over the spittle, and then I saw the praying mantis.

Version B
I had been ambling across this hill for several hours that day, when suddenly I noticed a speck of pure white. . . . I leaned to examine the white thing and [I] saw a mass of bubbles. It was <u>like spittle</u>. Then I saw something dark. It was <u>like an engorged leech</u>. It was rummaging over the spittle, and then I saw the praying mantis.

Exercise 7. Coordinate Structures and Discourse Effects

The following two passages are from Ernest Hemingway novels. Passage 1 is one of the excerpts discussed in the textbook (chap. 8) from *The Old Man and the Sea,* and passage 2 is from *For Whom the Bell Tolls.* The narrator in the second passage is Robert Jordan, the protagonist in the novel. Compare these two passages, taking into account the coordinate structures in brackets. In your comparison, comment on the following.

(a) The type of scene being described in each passage
(b) The similarities and differences you find in particular discourse effects that seem to be, at least in part, enhanced by the use of various coordinate structures

(*Hint:* For (a), consider factors such as whether the scene depicted is one of external action or one of internal thoughts or states; for (b), whether time is seen as a simple sequencing of actions or events, as simultaneous actions or events, or as some combination of the two, etc.)

Passage 1

I hope I do not have to fight again, he thought. I hope so much that I do not have to fight again.

[But by midnight he fought] and [this time he knew the fight was useless]. [They came in a pack], and [he could only see the lines in the water that their fins made and their phosphorescence as they threw themselves on the fish]. He [clubbed at heads] and [heard (the jaws chop) and (the shaking of the skiff)] as they took hold below. [He clubbed desperately at what he could only feel and hear] and [he felt something seize the club] and [it was gone]. . . .

[One came, finally, against the head itself] and [he knew that it was over]. . . . [He heard the tiller break] and [he lunged at the shark with the splintered butt]. [He felt it go in] and [knowing it was sharp he drove it in again]. The shark [let go] and [rolled away]. That was the last shark of the pack that came. There was nothing more for them to eat.

Passage 2

[He was walking beside her] but [his mind was thinking of the problem of the bridge now] and [it was all (clear and hard and sharp)] as when a camera lens is brought into focus. He saw [the two posts and Anselmo and the gypsy watching]. [He saw the road empty] and [he saw movement on it]. . . . He [placed the charges, wedged and lashed them], [sunk his caps and crimped them], [ran his wires, hooked them up and got back to where he had placed the old box of the exploder] and [then he started to think of all the things that could have happened and that might go wrong]. Stop it, he told himself.

Exercise 8. Subordinate Structures and Discourse Effects

This passage is also an excerpt from Ernest Hemingway's *For Whom the Bell Tolls,* and the narrator is again Robert Jordan. Compare this passage with those in exercise 7, noting any differences in types of structures that seem to predominate overall. In your comparison, comment on the following.

(a) The type of scene being described in passage 3 compared with the passages in exercise 7

(b) The similarities or differences you find in particular discourse effects that seem to be achieved, at least in part, by the use of various subordinate structures, as compared with coordinate structures

Be sure to take into account differences in the types of scenes being depicted, such as a series of actions or simultaneous events versus mental states, philosophical musings, and so on.

Passage 3

Bigotry is an odd thing. [To be bigoted] you have to be absolutely sure that you are right [and nothing makes that surety and righteousness like continence]. Continence is the foe of heresy.

How would that premise stand up [if he examined it]? That was probably [why the Communists were always cracking down on Bohemianism]. [When you were drunk] or [when you committed (either fornication or adultery)] you recognized your own personal fallibility of that so mutable substitute for the apostles' creed, the party line. Down with Bohemianism, the sin of Mayakovsky.

Chapter 9

Relative Clauses and Other Complex Noun Structures

Exercise 1. Restrictive and Nonrestrictive Relative Clauses

In the following passage, distinguish the bracketed relative clauses as restrictive or nonrestrictive by writing R or N in the blanks at the end. The passage is from Sherwood Anderson's story "The Egg."

> One unversed in such matters can have no notion of the many tragic things (1) [that can happen to a chicken]. It is born out of an egg, lives for a few weeks as a tiny fluffy thing such as you will see pictured on Easter cards, then becomes hideously naked, eats quantities of corn and meal bought by the sweat of your father's brow, gets diseases . . . stands looking with stupid eyes at the sun, becomes sick and dies. A few hens and now and then a rooster, (2) [which are intended to serve God's mysterious ends], struggle through to maturity. The hens lay eggs (3) [out of which come other chickens] and the dreadful cycle is thus made complete. It is all unbelievably complex. Small chickens, (4) [which are just setting out on the journey of life], look so bright and alert and they are in fact so dreadfully stupid. . . . In later life I have seen how a literature has been built up on the subject of fortunes to be made out of the raising of chickens. It is intended to be read by the gods (5) [who have just eaten of the tree of knowledge of good and evil]. . . . Do not be led astray by it.

1. __   4. __

2. __   5. __

3. __

Exercise 2. Relative Pronoun Case

In the following passage, from *In Search of Our Mothers' Gardens: Womanist Prose*, by Alice Walker, choose the appropriate forms of the relative pronouns from the list and write them in the blanks following the passage.

who   which
whom   that
whose

I am twelve. When relatives come to visit I hide in my room. My cousin Brenda, just my age, (1) _____ father works in the post office and (2) _____ mother is a nurse, comes to find me. "Hello," she says. And then she asks, looking at my recent school picture, (3) _____ I did not want taken, and on (4) _____ the "glob," as I think of it, is clearly visible, "You still can't see out of that eye?" . . .

I am fourteen and babysitting for my brother Bill, (5) _____ lives in Boston. He is my favorite brother and there is a strong bond between us. Understanding my feelings of shame and ugliness he and his wife take me to a local hospital, where the "glob" is removed. . . . There is still a small bluish crater where the scar tissue was, but the ugly white stuff is gone. Almost immediately I become a different person from the girl (6) _____ does not raise her head. Or so I think. . . . Now that I've raised my head I have plenty of friends . . . and I leave high school as valedictorian, most popular student, and *queen,* hardly believing my luck. Ironically, the girl (7) _____ was voted most beautiful in our class (and was) was later shot twice through the chest by a male companion . . . while she was pregnant. But that's another story in itself. Or is it?

1. _____   5. _____

2. _____   6. _____

3. _____   7. _____

4. _____

Exercise 3. Optional/Obligatory Relative Pronouns

In the following passage, indicate whether the underlined relative pronouns are optional or obligatory by writing OPT or OBL in the corresponding blanks following the passage (see especially chap. 9 in the textbook, section 9.4.4). The passage is from Gloria Steinem's essay "Ruth's Song (Because She Could Not Sing It)."

The nurses let my sister and me stay in the room long after there was no more breath. She had asked us to do that. One of her many fears came from a story (1) <u>that</u> she had been told as a child about a man (2) <u>whose</u> coma was mistaken for death. . . .

Her memorial service was in the Episcopalian church (3) <u>that</u> she loved because it fed the poor. . . . Most of all, she loved the affection with (4) <u>which</u> its members had welcomed her, visited her at home, and driven her to services. I think she would have liked the Quaker-style informality with (5) <u>which</u> people rose to tell their memories of her. I know she would have loved the presence of many friends. It was to this church that she donated some of her remaining Michigan property in the hope that it could be used as a multiracial camp, thus getting even with those people in the tiny nearby town (6) <u>who</u> had snubbed my father for being Jewish.

1. _____   4. _____

2. _____   5. _____

3. _____   6. _____

Exercise 4. Distinguishing Postnominal Clause Functions

In the following passage, distinguish relative clauses from appositive clauses by writing REL or APP in the blanks at the end. The passage is from Sherwood Anderson's "The Egg."

For ten years my father and mother struggled to make our chicken farm pay and then they gave up that struggle and began another. They moved into the town of Bidwell.

We must have been a sad looking lot, not, I fancy, unlike refugees fleeing from a battlefield. Mother and I walked in the road. The wagon (1) [that contained our goods] had been borrowed for the day from Mr. Albert Griggs, a neighbor. Out of its sides stuck the legs of cheap chairs and at the back of the pile of beds, tables, and boxes . . . was a crate of live chickens, and on top of that the baby carriage (2) [in which I had been wheeled about in my infancy]. Why we stuck to the baby carriage I don't know. People (3) [who have few possessions] cling tightly to those (4) [they have]. That is one of the facts (5) [that make life so discouraging].

Father rode on top of the wagon. He was then a bald-headed man of forty-five. . . . All during our ten years on the chicken farm he had worked as a laborer on neighboring farms and most of the money (6) [he had earned] had been spent for remedies to cure chicken diseases, on Wilmer's White Wonder Cholera or Professor Bidlow's Egg Producer or some other preparations (7) [that mother found advertised in the poultry papers].

Grotesques are born out of eggs as out of people. . . . A chicken is, you see, born (8) [that has four legs, two pairs of wings, two heads or what not]. The things do not live. . . . The fact (9) [that the poor little things could not live] was one of the tragedies of life to father. He had some sort of notion (10) [that his fortune would be made] if he could but bring into henhood or roosterhood a five-legged hen or a two-headed rooster. He dreamed of taking the wonder about to county fairs and of growing rich by exhibiting it to other farm-hands.

1. _____   6. _____

2. _____   7. _____

3. _____   8. _____

4. _____   9. _____

5. _____   10. _____

Exercise 5. Distinguishing Relative, Nominal, and Appositive Clauses

In the following passage, from Toni Cade Bambara's "The Hammer Man," in her collection of stories *Gorilla, My Love,* identify the bracketed clauses as relative, nominal, or appositive clauses by writing REL, NOM, or APP in the blanks following the passage.

I was glad to hear (1) [that Manny had fallen off the roof]. I had put out the tale (2) [that I was down with yellow fever], but nobody paid me no mind, least of all Dirty Red, who stomped right in to announce (3) [that Manny had fallen off the roof and that I could come out of hiding now]. My mother dropped (4) [what she was doing], (5) [which was the laundry], and got the whole story out of Red. "Bad enough you gots to hang around with boys," she said. "But fight with them too." . . .

I don't know (6) [how they got Manny on the roof finally]. . . .

Then one night I'm walking past the Douglas Street park . . . and there's ole Manny on the basketball court. . . . Being me, I quite naturally walk right up and ask (7) [what the hell he's doing playing in the dark]. . . . And then a squad car pulled up and a short cop with hair like one of the Marx Brothers came out hitching up his pants. He looked real hard at me and then at Manny.

"What are you two doing?" . . .

And I'm standing there thinking (8) [that none of my teachers . . . knew what they were talking about]. I'll be damned if I ever knew one of them rosy-cheeked cops (9) [that smiled and helped you get to school] without you or your little raggedy dog getting hit by a truck (10) [that had a smile on its face, too].

1. _____   6. _____

2. _____   7. _____

3. _____   8. _____

4. _____   9. _____

5. _____   10. _____

Exercise 6. Functions of *That* Clauses: Relative, Appositive, and Nominal

As discussed in chapters 8 and 9 in the textbook, there are three types of clauses beginning with the word *that:* relative, appositive, and nominal. (In relative clauses, *that* functions as a relative pronoun; in appositive or nominal clauses it functions simply as an introductory word.) In the following passage, identify each bracketed clause by writing REL, APP, or NOM in the blanks at the end. The passage is from *The Great Eskimo Vocabulary Hoax and Other Irreverent Essays on the Study of Language,* by Geoffrey K. Pullum.

Once the public has decided to accept something as an interesting fact, it becomes almost impossible to get the acceptance rescinded. . . . For instance, the notion (1) [that dinosaurs were stupid, slow-moving reptiles] (2) [that soon died out] because they were unsuccessful and couldn't keep up with the industrious mammals is stuck in the public consciousness. . . . No one wants to hear (3) [that the dinosauria dominated the planet with intelligence and adaptive genius for hundreds of millions of years]. . . .

But sadly, the academic profession shows a strong tendency to create stable and self-sustaining but completely false legends of its own. . . . In the study of language, one case surpasses all others in its degree of ubiquity. . . . It is the notion (4) [that Eskimos have bucketloads of different words for snow]. . . .

But the truth is (5) [that the Eskimos do not have lots of different words for snow], and no one who knows anything about . . . languages spoken by Eskimos . . . has ever said (6) [that they do]. Anyone who insists on simply checking their primary sources will find (7) [that they are quite unable to document the alleged facts about snow vocabulary] (but nobody ever checks, because the truth might not be what the reading public wants to hear).

1. _____   5. _____

2. _____   6. _____

3. _____   7. _____

4. _____

Exercise 7. Prepositional Phrase Functions: Postnominals versus Adverbials

As seen in earlier chapters, prepositional phrases function as different types of modifiers. One important function is adverbial, and another is postnominal modifier. The difference between these functions of prepositional phrases is illustrated in the following passage from Scott Sanders's essay "Listening to Owls," repeated from chapter 3 in the textbook. Identify the functions of the prepositional phrases in brackets either as adverbials or as postnominal modifiers by writing ADV or POSTNOM in the blanks following the passage.

> As the light grew stronger, we noticed that near the lake's edge the black ice was covered with a rough, white fur. When we were closer, we could see that the fur was really a miniature forest (1) [of ice crystals], each crystal fern-shaped, a tiny glistening lattice. . . . The tallest thicket (2) [of crystals] was no higher than the knuckle on a flattened hand, yet within those pygmy thickets there was more intricacy than the eye could follow. . . . The light shattered (3) [on the crystals] as I gently twirled the stem (4) [of a foxtail grass]; a sliver (5) [of ice], thinner than an eyelash, broke (6) [from a hydrogen explosion] (7) [into rainbows]. Soon the frost (8) [on my foxtail] melted. Before my very eyes the ice forest was evaporating (9) [from the margins] (10) [of the lake], a disappearing trick more astonishing than any Saturday afternoon magic.

1. _____   6. _____

2. _____   7. _____

3. _____   8. _____

4. _____   9. _____

5. _____   10. _____

Exercise 8. Appositive Phrases

Indicate whether the bracketed appositives in the following passage are restrictive (R) or nonrestrictive (N) by writing the appropriate letters in the blanks following the passage. (*Hint:* Relevant punctuation has been omitted; therefore, it should help to consider in each case whether punctuation—either comma or semicolon—is necessary.) The passage is from "My Oedipus Complex," by Frank O'Connor.

> Father was in the army all through the war. Like Santa Claus he came and went mysteriously. He smoked cigarettes (1) [a habit that gave him a pleasantly musty smell] and shaved his beard (2) [an operation of astounding interest to me]. Each time he left a trail of souvenirs (3) [model tanks and Gurkha knives with handles made of bullet cases, and German helmets and cap badges and button-sticks, and all sorts of military equipment] (4) [all of it carefully stowed away in a long box on top of the wardrobe], in case they ever came in handy. I sometimes thought of him as my father (5) [the magpie]; he expected everything to come in handy.

1. __   4. __

2. __   5. __

3. __

Exercise 9. Recognizing Postnominal Structures and Functions

In the following passage, first identify each bracketed structure by writing the corresponding number in the blank in the first column following the passage. Use the numbers in the list. Then identify the function of each as restrictive or nonrestrictive by writing R or N in the blank in the second column. The passage is from Saul Bellow's novel *Henderson the Rain King*.

(1) Relative clause
(2) Appositive clause
(3) Appositive phrase

> The man who kept us waiting, (1) [the black Wariri magistrate . . .], was letting us cool our bottoms. . . . As I was sitting waiting here on this exotic night I bit into a hard biscuit and I broke one of my bridges.

After this I was compelled to recall the history of my dental work. The first major job was undertaken . . . , in Paris, by Mlle. Montecuccoli.

The second bridge, (2) [the one I had just broken with the hardtack], was made in New York by . . . Doctor Spohr, (3) [who was first cousin to Klaus Spohr], (4) [the painter who was doing Lily's portrait]. While I was in the dentist's chair, Lily was sitting for the artist. . . . The picture of her was a cause of trouble between me and my eldest son, (5) [Edward]. He is like his mother and thinks himself better than me. Well, he's wrong. Great things are done by Americans but not by the likes of either of us. They are done by people like that man (6) [Slocum], (7) [who builds the great dams]. . . . That's the type (8) [that gets things done]. On this my class, (9) [the class (that) Lily was so eager to marry into], gets zero. Edward has always gone with the crowd. The most independent thing (10) [that he ever did] was to dress up a chimpanzee in a cowboy suit and drive it around New York in his open car.

Structure	Function
1. ___	1. ___
2. ___	2. ___
3. ___	3. ___
4. ___	4. ___
5. ___	5. ___
6. ___	6. ___
7. ___	7. ___
8. ___	8. ___
9. ___	9. ___
10. ___	10. ___

Chapter 10

Nonfinite Clause Constructions

Exercise 1. Recognizing Finite and Nonfinite Clauses

In the following passage, from Roger Angell's essay on Stephen Crane, "The Greatest of the Boys," identify each clause in brackets as either finite or nonfinite by writing either F or N in the blanks following the passage.

I had read the assigned stuff in school: *Maggie: A Girl of the Streets,* a tenement novella (1) [delivered in distractingly literal Bowery-ese] *[Past part.]* *[Adv.]* *[Object of prep.]* about lives (2) [made glum by poverty and booze], . . . and the obligatory *Red Badge of Courage,* (3) [which presented the soldier's war as one of stupefying boredom] (4) [interrupted by incomprehensible events and outbursts of terror]. . . . *Past part.* *Adjectival (relative)*

No doubt like other men of my generation, . . . I can recall sometimes (5) [thinking back on Crane's battle scenes] while I was in college, . . . and wondering (6) [how I would perform] (7) [when it came time for me to be in combat]. . . . Another war was coming . . . and we needed (8) [to get ready for it]. . . .

With Vietnam, the iconography of war shifted . . . to something smaller and more intimately bloody. . . . The Keatsian glimmer (9) [that enfolded Crane after his early death] is less interesting than his own aura. (10) [Barely matriculating into our century], never able to match the achievement of his first success, (11) [he feels locked away within his youth], in an America (12) [that has not quite grown up yet, either].

1. N   7. F
2. N   8. N
3. F   9. F
4. N   10. N
5. N   11. F
6. F   12. F

finite clause needs subj.

non finite {
participle = present + past
to + verb
gerund (ing) - acting as noun

Exercise 2. Recognizing Types of Nonfinite Clauses

In this passage, adapted from Deirdre McNamer's novel *Rima in the Weeds*, repeated from chapter 1, the bracketed structures include infinitive, gerund, and participial clauses. Identify each bracketed structure according to type by writing the corresponding abbreviations in the blanks following the passage. Use the abbreviations in the list.

INF   (Infinitive) *to + verb*
BARE INF   (Bare infinitive) *verb*
GER   (Gerund) *-ing – nominal*
PART   (Participial) *-ed/en*
                            adverbial, relatively

(1) [To raise money that spring], Margaret's catechism class sold plastic cylinders with a figure of the Virgin Mary inside. They were beige and looked like foot-long rockets. . . . Anyone who sold three of them got (2) [to name an African Pagan baby]. . . .

(3) [Trudging on Saturday mornings from door to door], (4) [selling the Virgin rockets], Margaret gathered evidence of something she already felt in her bones—that Madrid . . . was not just a gappy little town on the northern Montana plains. Far from it, it was a place of layers and mysteries, of hidden rooms and muffled dramas. . . .

(5) [Selling the rockets], she saw, through a slat in a venetian blind, an old man in red boxer shorts (6) [vacuuming a carpet]. She heard Mr. Badenoch, the meek grade school principal, (7) [singing in a heartbreaking voice from beneath a car in his garage], and she watched a three-legged dog with a bow on its collar (8) [hop through a tunnel in some bushes].

1. _Infinitive_   5. _participial (adverbial – modifying whole sentence)_
2. _Infinitive_   6. _participial_
3. _participial_   7. _participial_
4. _participial_   8. _bare infinitive_

Exercise 3. Logical Subjects in Infinitive Clauses

In this passage, blank slots have been left for the (logical) subjects of the infinitive clauses. Fill in the corresponding numbered blanks following the passage with the "logical" subject of the infinitive, that is, the person or persons who are to perform the action described by the infinitive verb (see chap. 10 in the textbook, section 10.1.3). Follow the example.

The passage is from the novel *Free Enterprise,* by Michelle Cliff. The narrator, a descendant of "feathered kings" of Hawai'i, is giving his account of the last moments of Captain Cook. The account is being retold through the words of his great-grandson.

> *Example:* (i) The natives want _____ to help you.
>
> (i) <u>the natives</u>

At first I liked James Cook. He seemed like a fair man, a technician rather than an ideologue—at first. . . .

A few of the younger men took a longboat from the side of the *Discovery.* Their intention was (1) _____ to decorate the boat with carving, commemorating Cook's visit to the islands. In so doing we would celebrate his departure . . . at the same time we would honor him. It is our custom, as you know, (2) _____ to give a gift, a memento, to see someone on his way. . . .

We were eager for his departure. Too many liberties taken, for one thing. . . . We could sense what was coming. We wanted (3) _____ to avoid bloodshed, which bloodshed was becoming inevitable with our growing realization that these Englishmen did not simply wish (4) _____ to visit us, to "discover" us, as they put it. They wanted (5) _____ to own us, and the islands. . . .

So we decided (6) _____ to send them on their way, in celebration with feasting, and let the Maori take care of them. . . .

James Cook made a serious mistake. He returned to us. The journey on which he lost his life was his second journey to Hawai'i, which, in homage to his patron, he had christened the Sandwich Islands. You might well laugh, given our reputation, well earned, for anthropophagy.

1. _____   4. _____

2. _____   5. _____

3. _____   6. _____

Exercise 4. Logical Subjects of Infinitives, Gerunds, and Participials

In this passage, from Barbara Kingsolver's novel *The Bean Trees,* blank slots have been left for the (logical) subjects of the infinitive, gerundive, and participial clauses. Fill in the corresponding numbered blanks following the passage with the "logical" subject of the infinitive, gerund, or participial, that is, the person or persons who are to perform the action described by the verb (see chap. 10 in the textbook, section 10.1.3). Follow the example.

Example: (i) That was Mama for you, _____ always bragging about her little girl.
(i) <u>Mama</u>

Missy was what everyone called me . . . because when I was three supposedly I stamped my foot and told my own mother not (1) _____ to call me Marietta, but *Miss* Marietta . . . and so she did from that day forward. Miss Marietta and later on just Missy.

The thing you have to understand is, it was just like Mama (2) _____ to do that. When I was just the littlest kid I would go pond fishing of a Sunday and bring home the boniest mess of bluegills and maybe a bass the size of your thumb, and the way Mama would carry on you would think I'd caught the famous big lunker. . . . "That's my big girl, (3) _____ bringing home the bacon," she would say, and cook those things and serve them up like Thanksgiving for the two of us.

I loved (4) _____ fishing those old mud-bottomed ponds. Partly because she would be proud of whatever I dragged out, but also I just loved (5) _____ sitting still. You could smell leaves, (6) _____ rotting into the cool mud, and watch the Jesus bugs walk on the water, their four little feet making dents in the surface but never falling through. And sometimes you'd see the big ones, the ones nobody was ever going (7) _____ to hook, (8) _____ slipping away under the water like dark-brown dreams.

1. _____

2. _____

3. _____

4. _____

5. _____

6. _____

7. _____

8. _____

Exercise 5. Distinguishing Clause Categories

Read the passage repeated from exercise 1, from Roger Angell's essay on Stephen Crane, "The Greatest of the Boys." Identify the clause categories by writing the corresponding abbreviations in the blanks following the passage. Use the abbreviations in the list.

Clause Types   nonfinite
Main   (MAIN)   Infinitive   (INF)
Adverbial   (ADV)   Gerundive   (GER)
Relative   (REL)   Participial   (PART)
Nominal   (NOM)
(finite)

I had read the assigned stuff in school: *Maggie: A Girl of the Streets,* a tenement novella (1) [delivered in distractingly literal Bowery-ese] about lives (2) [made glum by poverty and booze], . . . and the obligatory *Red Badge of Courage,* (3) [which presented the soldier's war as one of stupefying boredom] (4) [interrupted by incomprehensible events and outbursts of terror]. . . .

No doubt like other men of my generation, . . . I can recall sometimes (5) [thinking back on Crane's battle scenes] while I was in college, . . . and wondering (6) [how I would perform] (7) [when it came time for me to be in combat]. . . . Another war was coming . . . and we needed (8) [to get ready for it]. . . .

With Vietnam, the iconography of war shifted . . . to something smaller and more intimately bloody. . . . The Keatsian glimmer (9) [that enfolded Crane after his early death] is less interesting than his own aura. relat. pro. (10) [Barely matriculating into our century], never able to match the achievement of his first success, (11) [he feels locked away within his youth], in an America (12) [that has not quite grown up yet, either].

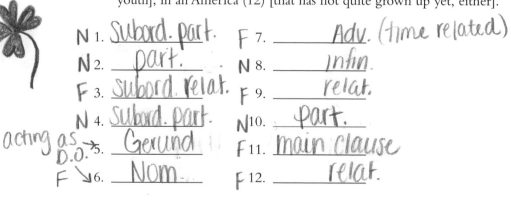

N 1. Subord. part.   F 7. _____Adv. (time related)
N 2. _____part._____   N 8. _____Infin.
F 3. Subord. relat.   F 9. _____relat.
N 4. Subord. part.   N 10. _____part.
acting as → 5. Gerund   F 11. main clause
D.O.
F → 6. Nom.   F 12. _____relat.

Exercise 6. Restrictive versus Nonrestrictive Postnominal Participials

Identify the adjectival function of the postnominal participials following as either restrictive or nonrestrictive by writing either R or N in the blanks following the passage. The excerpt is from Sherwood Anderson's story "Mother," in his book *Winesburg, Ohio*.

Elizabeth Willard, the mother of George Willard, was a tall, gaunt woman with a face (1) [marked by smallpox scars]. Although she was but forty-five, some obscure disease had taken the fire out of her figure. Listlessly she went about the disorderly old hotel, looking at the faded wallpaper and the ragged carpets, doing the work of a chambermaid among beds (2) [soiled by the slumbers of fat traveling men]. Her husband, Tom Willard, a slender, graceful man with square shoulders, a quick military step, and black mustache, (3) [trained to turn sharply up at the ends], tried to put the wife out of his mind. The presence of the tall ghostly figure, (4) [moving slowly through the halls], he took as a reproach to himself. . . . He thought of the old house and the woman who lived there with him as things (5) [defeated and done for]. The hotel in which he had begun his life so hopefully was now a mere ghost of what a hotel should be.

1. __   4. __

2. __   5. __

3. __

Exercise 7. Recognizing Functions of Nonfinite Clauses

In the following paragraph, the bracketed structures include infinitive, gerund, and participial clauses. The functions of these clauses vary depending on their use in the discourse. Read the following passage adapted from Saul Bellow's novel *Herzog* and identify the function of each clause by writing the corresponding abbreviations in the blanks following the passage. Use the abbreviations in the list.

Functions (Infinitives and Gerunds)
Nominal function   (NOM)
Postnominal modifier   (POSTNOM MOD)
Complement (of adjective) (ADJC)

Functions (Participials)

Adjectival	(ADJ)
Adverbial	(ADV)

Professor Herzog had the unconscious frankness of a man (1) [deeply preoccupied]. And toward the end of the term there were long pauses in his lectures. He would stop, (2) [muttering "Excuse me,"] (3) [reaching inside his coat for his pen]. The table creaking, he wrote on scraps of paper with a great pressure of eagerness in his hand; he was absorbed, his eyes darkly circled. . . .

(4) [Lying on the sofa of the kitchenette apartment he had rented], . . . he went on (5) [taking stock]. . . . Was he a clever man or an idiot? Well, he could not at this time claim (6) [to be clever]. The sharpies had cleaned him out. . . . He was losing his hair. He read the ads of the Thomas Scalp Specialists, with the exaggerated skepticism of a man whose craving (7) [to believe] was deep, desperate. Scalp Experts! . . .

(8) [Satisfied with his own severity], (9) [positively enjoying the hardness and factual rigor of his judgement], he lay on his sofa. . . .

Herzog made a fresh start in life. With twenty thousand dollars (10) [inherited from his charming father], he quit an academic position and bought a big old house. . . . In the peaceful Berkshires . . . it should be easy (11) [to write his second volume on the social ideas of the Romantics].

1. _____	7. _____
2. _____	8. _____
3. _____	9. _____
4. _____	10. _____
5. _____	11. _____
6. _____	

Exercise 8. Participials and Discourse Effects

In this passage, the excerpt from Saul Bellow's novel *Herzog* given in exercise 7 has been rewritten with some of the participial clauses revised as unreduced, finite clauses. Compare the original participials in exercise 7 with the rewritten clauses in the brackets and comment on any differences you see in discourse effects, such as differences in the variety and effectiveness of expression, in focusing attention on certain parts over others, in the rhythm and flow of the discourse, or in other stylistic effects you may find.

Professor Herzog had the unconscious frankness of a man (1) [who was deeply preoccupied]. And toward the end of the term there were long pauses in his lectures. He would stop, (2) [at which time he would mutter "Excuse me,"] (3) [while he would reach inside his coat for his pen]. (4) [While the table creaked], he wrote on scraps of paper with a great pressure of eagerness in his hand; he was absorbed, his eyes darkly circled. . . .

(5) [While he was lying on the sofa of the kitchenette apartment he had rented] . . . he went on taking stock. . . . Was he a clever man or an idiot? Well, he could not at this time claim to be clever. The sharpies had cleaned him out. . . . He was losing his hair. He read the ads of the Thomas Scalp Specialists, with the exaggerated skepticism of a man whose craving to believe was deep, desperate. Scalp Experts! . . .

(6) (A man) [who was satisfied with his own severity], (7) (a man) [who was positively enjoying the hardness and factual rigor of his judgement], he lay on his sofa. . . .

Herzog made a fresh start in life. With twenty thousand dollars (8) [that he had inherited from his charming father], he quit an academic position and bought a big old house. . . . In the peaceful Berkshires . . . it should be easy to write his second volume on the social ideas of the Romantics.

Chapter 11
Information Packaging

Exercise 1. Theme and Focus

Read again the brief excerpt from Ernest Hemingway's novel *The Old Man and the Sea* discussed in chapter 1 in the textbook and respond to the questions that follow.

> It was on the third turn that he saw the fish first. . . . (1) On this circle <u>the old man</u> <u>could see the fish's eye and the two gray sucking fish that swam around him</u>. (2) Sometimes <u>they</u> <u>attached themselves to him</u>. (3) Sometimes <u>they</u> <u>darted off</u>. (4) Sometimes <u>they</u> <u>would swim easily in his shadow</u>.

(a) For the numbered sentences (1) through (4), discuss the underlined subjects and predicates with respect to the correspondence of given/new information and theme/focus positions.

(b) Do the pronouns in the subject positions of (2), (3), and (4) correspond to the discourse expectations set up by sentence (1)? Explain.

Exercise 2. Theme and Focus: Cleft Sentences

Discuss the following cleft sentence, adapted from the excerpt from Steven G. Kellman's review article "Camus the African" that appears in chapter 9 in the textbook, in terms of given/new information and the focusing function of cleft structures.

> It was Albert Camus who was the first African author to win the Nobel Prize, not Wole Soyinka.

Exercise 3. Preposed Sentence Adverbials

The following passage, repeated from chapter 3 of the textbook, is from the novel *All the Pretty Horses* by Cormac McCarthy. In this excerpt a captain in a Mexican jail is questioning a prisoner, the protagonist in the novel. Read the passage and respond to the questions that follow.

You have the opportunity to tell the truth <u>here</u>. <u>Here</u>. In three days you will go to Saltillo and <u>then</u> you will [not] have this opportunity. It will be gone. <u>Then</u> the truth will be in other hands. You see. We can make the truth <u>here</u>. Or we can lose it. But when you leave it <u>here</u> it will be <u>too late</u>. <u>Too late</u> for truth. <u>Then</u> you will be in the hands of other parties. Who can say what the truth will be <u>then</u>? At that time? <u>Then</u> you will blame yourself. You will see.

Discuss the adverbials in this passage. Compare those in final position (normal word order) with those preposed to initial position. Base your discussion on the discourse effects of the varying adverbial positions in sentences throughout the passage. (See also chap. 3 on the cumulative effect of the repetition of the adverbs *here* and *then*.)

Exercise 4. Preposed Elements and Inversion

The following excerpt is from the opening scene of Thornton Wilder's play *Our Town*. Read the excerpt and respond to the questions that follow.

A longer version of this passage was discussed in chapter 7 of the textbook. Recall that the Stage Manager enters and places a table and three chairs downstage left and a similar arrangement downstage right. The narration is by the Stage Manager.

Well, I'd better show you how our town lies. <u>Up here</u>—
(That is: parallel with the back wall.)
[<u>is</u> <u>Main Street</u>]. Way back there is the railway station; tracks go that way. Polish Town's across the tracks, and some Canuck families.
(Toward the left.)
<u>Over there</u> [<u>is</u> <u>the Congregational Church</u>]; <u>across the</u> <u>street</u>'[<u>s</u> <u>the Presbyterian</u>].
Methodist and Unitarian are over there.

Comment on the discourse effects of the preposed adverbials (underlined) in combination with the inverted subject and verb (underlined and bracketed).

Exercise 5. Comparing Preposed Adverbial Structures

This excerpt is from the opening passage of Joseph Conrad's novel *The Secret Sharer* (see also chap. 7 in the textbook). Read the passage and respond to the questions that follow.

(1) [On my right hand] there were lines of fishing-stakes resembling a mysterious system of half-submerged bamboo fences. . . . There was no sign of human habitation as far as the eye could reach. (2) [To the left] a group of barren islets, suggesting ruins of stone walls, towers, and blockhouses, had its foundations set in a blue sea that itself looked solid, so still and stable did it lie below my feet. . . . . (3) [And when I turned my head to take a parting glance at the tug which had just left us anchored outside the bar], I saw the straight line of the flat shore joined to the stable sea, edge to edge, with a perfect and unmarked closeness, in one levelled floor half brown, half blue under the enormous dome of the sky.

Compare the preposed adverbial phrases in (1) and (2) and the preposed adverbial clause in (3). Comment on the discourse effects of each in terms of their preposed position in the sentence.

Exercise 6. Preposed Participial Clauses

Read the following passage, from N. Scott Momaday's book *The Way to Rainy Mountain,* and answer the questions that follow.

My grandmother had a reverence for the sun, a holy regard that now is all but gone out of mankind. . . . She was ten when the Kiowas came together for the last time as a living Sun Dance culture. They could find no buffalo; they had to hang an old hide from the sacred tree. Before the dance could begin, a company of soldiers rode out from Fort Sill under orders to disperse the tribe. (1) [Forbidden without cause the essential act of their faith], (2) [having seen the wild herds slaughtered and left to rot upon the ground], the Kiowas backed away forever from the medicine tree. That was July 20, 1890, at the great bend of the Washita. My grandmother was there. Without bitterness, and for as long as she lived, she bore a vision of deicide.

(1) Comment on the preposed participial clause labeled as (1) in terms of its position serving as a bridge from the content of previous discourse to the content of the main clause in the sentence. Take into account how the overall coherence of the paragraph might be affected if, instead, the main clause *the Kiowas backed away forever from the medicine tree* had been in the initial position in the sentence.
(2) Comment on the participial clause labeled as (2), taking the same factors into consideration.

Exercise 7. Preposed Elements and End Focus

Read the following passage, from N. Scott Momaday's book *The Way to Rainy Mountain,* repeated from exercise 6, and answer the question that follows.

> My grandmother had a reverence for the sun, a holy regard that now is all but gone out of mankind. . . . She was ten when the Kiowas came together for the last time as a living Sun Dance culture. They could find no buffalo; they had to hang an old hide from the sacred tree. Before the dance could begin, a company of soldiers rode out from Fort Sill under orders to disperse the tribe. Forbidden without cause the essential act of their faith, having seen the wild herds slaughtered and left to rot upon the ground, the Kiowas backed away forever from the medicine tree. That was July 20, 1890, at the great bend of the Washita. My grandmother was there. (1) [Without bitterness], (2) [and for as long as she lived], she bore a vision of deicide.

Discuss the preposed phrases in (1) and (2) in relation to the discourse effects not only of (i) positioning the word *deicide* in focus position in the sentence but also of (ii) positioning it as the final word of the entire paragraph.

Exercise 8. Preposed Parallel Elements and End Focus

In the following passage, from the famous essay by Martin Luther King, Jr., "Letter from Birmingham Jail," only two sentences have been excerpted (labeled A and B). Consider the series of preposed adverbial time clauses numbered (1)–(10) in sentence B and discuss the role of these clauses in (i) linking the content of this sentence to the preceding sentence A and in (ii) positioning the main clause in final position in sentence B. Take into consideration that the preposing of the time clauses in sentence B places the word *wait* in end focus position of the main clause, a position that is parallel to the end focus position of the word *wait* in sentence A.

> [A] Perhaps it is easy for those who have never felt the stinging darts of segregation to say, "Wait." [B] (1) [When you have seen vicious mobs lynch your mothers and fathers at will and drown your sisters and brothers at whim;] (2) [when you have seen hate-filled policemen curse, kick, and even kill your black brothers and sisters;] (3) [when you see the vast majority of your twenty million Negro brothers smothering in an airtight cage of poverty in the midst of an affluent society;] (4) [when you suddenly find your tongue twisted and your speech stammering as you

seek to explain to your six-year-old daughter why she can't go to the public amusement park that has just been advertised on television, and see tears welling up in her eyes when she is told that Funtown is closed to colored children, and see ominous clouds of inferiority beginning to form in her little mental sky, and see her beginning to distort her personality by developing an unconscious bitterness toward white people;] (5) [when you have to concoct an answer for a five-year-old son who is asking, "Daddy, why do white people treat colored people so mean?";] (6) [when you take a cross-country drive and find it necessary to sleep night after night in the uncomfortable corners of your automobile because no motel will accept you;] (7) [when you are humiliated day in and day out by nagging signs reading "white" and "colored";] (8) [when your first name becomes "nigger," your middle name becomes "boy" (however old you are) and your last name becomes "John," and your wife and mother are never given the respected title "Mrs.";] (9) [when you are harried by day and haunted by night by the fact that you are a Negro, living constantly at tiptoe stance, never quite knowing what to expect next, and are plagued with inner fears and outer resentments;] (10) [when you are forever fighting a degenerating sense of "nobodiness"]—[MAIN CLAUSE] then you will understand why we find it difficult to <u>wait</u>.

Selected Readings

Adams, Robert. "Soft Soap and the Nitty-Gritty." In *The Norton Reader: An Anthology of Expository Prose,* 7th ed., Arthur M. Eastman, Caesar R. Blake, Joan E. Hartman, Alan B. Howes, Robert T. Lenaghan, Leo F. McNamara, and James Rosier, 291, 295. New York: W. W. Norton and Company, 1988. First published in *Fair of Speech: The Uses of Euphemism, A Collection of Essays on Language,* ed. D. J. Enright (N.P., 1985).

Aiken, Conrad. "Impulse." In *Short Story Masterpieces,* ed. Robert Penn Warren and Albert Erskine, 15. New York: Dell Publishing Company, 1954.

Anderson, Sherwood. "The Egg." In *The Norton Anthology of American Literature,* 1743–45. New York: W. W. Norton and Company, 1989. First published in Sherwood Anderson, *The Triumph of the Egg.* New York: B. W. Huebach, 1921.

———. "Mother," from *Winesburg, Ohio.* In *The Norton Anthology of American Literature,* 1738. New York: W. W. Norton and Company, 1989. First published in the United States by Huebsch, 1919.

Angell, Roger. "The Greatest of the Boys." *New Yorker,* September 7, 1998, 85–86.

Angelou, Maya. *I Know Why the Caged Bird Sings,* 74–75. New York: Bantam Books, 1971.

Bambara, Toni Cade. "Hammer Man." In *Gorilla, My Love,* 35, 36, 39, 41–42. New York: Vintage Contemporaries, 1992.

Bellow, Saul. *Henderson the Rain King,* 102–3, 105–6. Greenwich, CT: Fawcett Publications, 1959.

———. *Herzog,* 2–5. New York: Viking Press, 1964.

Bierce, Ambrose. "An Occurrence at Owl Creek Bridge." In *The Norton Anthology of Short Fiction,* 4th ed., ed. R. V. Cassill, 100–101. New York: W. W. Norton and Company, 1990.

Campion, Jane, and Kate Pullinger. *The Piano,* 28–29. New York: Miramax Books, 1994.

Carroll, James. "An American Requiem." *Atlantic Monthly,* April 1996, 76.

Carter, Forrest. *The Education of Little Tree,* 47. Albuquerque: University of New Mexico Press, 1986.

Cather, Willa. *My Antonia,* 62–63. Boston: Houghton Mifflin Company, 1988.

Cisneros, Sandra. *The House on Mango Street,* 53–54. New York: Vintage Contemporaries, 1984.

Cliff, Michelle. *Free Enterprise,* 47–49. New York: Dutton Group USA, 1993.

Conrad, Joseph. *The Secret Sharer.* In *Heart of Darkness and The Secret Sharer: Joseph Conrad, The Complete Texts,* Bantam critical ed., 135. New York: Bantam Books, 1969.

Didion, Joan. "On Going Home," from *Slouching towards Bethlehem.* In *The Norton Reader: An Anthology of Expository Prose,* 9th ed., ed. Linda H. Peterson, Joan E. Hartman, and John C. Brereton, 56–59. New York: W. W. Norton and Company, 1996.

Dillard, Annie. "The Fixed," from *Pilgrim at Tinker Creek.* In *Ways of Reading,* ed. David Bartholomae and Anthony Petrosky, 157. New York: St. Martin's Press, 1987.

Eiseley, Loren. "The Brown Wasps." In *The Norton Reader: An Anthology of Expository Prose,* 7th ed., ed. Arthur M. Eastman, Caesar R. Blake, Hubert M. English, Jr., Joan E. Hartman, Alan B. Howes, Robert T. Lenaghan, Leo P. McNamara, and James Rosier, 72–73. New York: W. W. Norton and Company, 1988. First published in *The Night Country.* New York: Scribner, 1971.

Faulkner, William. *The Sound and the Fury,* 1–2. 1946. Reprint, New York: Random House, Vintage Books, 1946.

Frost, Robert. "Nothing Gold Can Stay." In *Selected Poems of Robert Frost,* 138. San Francisco, CA: Rinehart Press, 1963.

Golding, William. *The Inheritors.* New York: Harcourt Brace and World, 1955.

———. "Thinking as a Hobby." In *The Norton Reader: An Anthology of Expository Prose,* 7th ed., ed. Arthur M. Eastman, Caesar R. Blake, Hubert M. English, Jr., Joan E. Hartman, Alan B. Howes, Robert T. Lenaghan, Leo P. McNamara, and James Rosier, 173. New York: W. W. Norton and Company, 1988. First published in *Holiday Magazine.*

Guterson, David. *Snow Falling on Cedars,* 4–5. New York: Vintage Books, 1995.

Halliday, M. A. K. "Linguistic Function and Literary Style: An Inquiry into the Language of William Golding's *The Inheritors.*" In *Explorations in the Functions of Language,* 95–133. New York: Elsevier North Holland, 1975.

Hemingway, Ernest. *A Farewell to Arms.* In *Three Novels of Ernest Hemingway,* 112. New York: Charles Scribner's Sons, 1962.

———. *The Old Man and the Sea.* In *Three Novels of Ernest Hemingway.* New York: Charles Scribner's Sons, 1962.

———. *For Whom the Bell Tolls,* 177, 179–80. New York: Charles Scribner's Sons, 1940.

Henry, O. "A Municipal Report." In *Great American Short Stories,* ed. Wallace Stegner and Mary Stegner, 228. New York: Dell Publishing Company, 1957.

Hughes, Langston. "Salvation," from *The Big Sea.* In *The Norton Reader: An An-*

thology of Expository Prose, 9th ed., ed. Linda H. Peterson, Joan E. Hartman, and John C. Brereton, 1199–1201. New York: W. W. Norton and Company, 1996.

James, Henry. *Daisy Miller.* In *The Literature of the United States,* 3d ed., ed. Walter Blair, Theodore Hornberger, Randall Stewart, and James E. Miller, Jr., 496–97, 499–500, 529–30, 535–36. Glenview, IL: Scott, Foresman and Company, 1953.

Johnson, Diane. "Great Barrier Reef." In *Best American Short Stories,* ed. Louise Erdrich and Katrina Kenison, 286–87. Boston and New York: Houghton Mifflin Company, 1993.

Kesey, Ken. *Sometimes a Great Notion.* New York: Bantam Books, 1964, 45–46.

King, Martin Luther, Jr., "Letter from Birmingham Jail," from *Why We Can't Wait.* New York: Harper and Row, 1964. In *The Norton Reader: An Anthology of Expository Prose,* 9th ed., ed. Linda H. Peterson, Joan E. Hartman, and John C. Brereton, 886–900. New York: W. W. Norton and Company, 1996.

Kingsolver, Barbara. *The Bean Trees,* 2. New York: Harper and Row, 1988.

Kuhn, Thomas. "The Historical Structure of Scientific Discovery." In *Ways of Reading,* ed. David Bartholomae and Anthony Petrosky, 339–40. New York: St. Martin's Press, 1987.

Lardner, Ring. "Who Dealt?" In *The Oxford Book of Short Stories,* ed. V. S. Pritchett, 292. New York: Oxford University Press, 1981.

LeGuin, Ursula K. *The Lathe of Heaven,* 7. New York: Avon Books, 1973. First published in *Amazing Stories Magazine,* 1971.

Malcolm, Janet. "A House of One's Own." *New Yorker,* June 5, 1995, 58, 78.

Maugham, W. Somerset. "The Outstation." In *Short Story Masterpieces,* ed. Robert Penn Warren and Albert Erskine, 289. New York: Dell Publishing Company, 1954. First published in *The Casuarina Tree,* 1926.

McCarthy, Cormac. *All the Pretty Horses,* 168. New York: Vintage Books, 1993.

———. *Suttree,* 10–11. New York: Vintage International Books, 1992.

McNamer, Deirdre. *Rima in the Weeds,* 6–7. New York: HarperCollins Publishers, 1991.

Miller, Arthur. *The Last Yankee.* In *The Best American Short Plays: 1991–1992,* ed. Howard Stein and Glenn Young, 137–38. New York: Applause Theatre Books, 1992.

Momaday, N. Scott. Excerpt from *The Way to Rainy Mountain,* 10. Albuquerque: University of New Mexico Press, 1969.

Mori, Kyoko. "Yellow Mittens and Early Violets." In *The Forbidden Stitch: An Asian American Women's Anthology,* ed. Shirley Geok-lin Lim, Mayumi Tsutakawa, and Margarita Donnelly, 31. Corvallis, OR: Calyx Books, 1989.

Morrison, Toni. *Beloved,* 205, 207–8. New York: Alfred A. Knopf, 1987.

———. *The Bluest Eye,* 52. New York: Washington Square Press, 1970.

Narayan, R. K. "A Horse and Two Goats." In *The Oxford Book of Short Stories,* ed. V. S. Pritchett, 404. New York: Oxford University Press, 1981. From *A Horse and Two Goats* (Bodley Head, 1970).

O'Connor, Frank. "My Oedipus Complex." In *Short Story Masterpieces,* ed. Robert Penn Warren and Albert Erskine, 350. New York: Dell Publishing Company, 1954.

O'Flaherty, Liam. "The Tent." In *The Oxford Book of Short Stories,* ed. V. S. Pritchett, 322–29. New York: Oxford University Press, 1981.

Porter, Katherine Anne. "Flowering Judas." In *The Literature of the United States,* 3d ed., ed. Walter Blair, Theodore Hornberger, Randall Stewart, and James E. Miller, Jr., 1195–96. Glenview, IL: Scott, Foresman and Company, 1953.

Pullum, Geoffrey K. *The Great Eskimo Vocabulary Hoax and Other Irreverent Essays on the Study of Language,* 159–60. Chicago: University of Chicago Press, 1991.

Rhys, Jean. *Wide Sargasso Sea,* 104, 107–8. New York: W. W. Norton and Company, 1982.

Sanders, Scott. "Listening to Owls." In *The Norton Reader: An Anthology of Expository Prose,* 7th ed., ed. Arthur M. Eastman, Caesar R. Blake, Hubert M. English, Jr., Joan E. Hartman, Alan B. Howes, Robert T. Lenaghan, Leo F. McNamara, and James Rosier, 59–60. New York: W. W. Norton and Company, 1988. First published in *North American Review,* March 1982.

Sarton, May. *Journal of a Solitude,* 384–93. New York: W. W. Norton and Co., 1973. In *The Norton Reader: An Anthology of Expository Prose,* 9th ed., ed. Linda H. Peterson, Joan E. Hartman, and John C. Brereton, 118. New York: W. W. Norton and Company, 1996.

Steinem, Gloria. "Ruth's Song (Because She Could Not Sing It)." In *The Winchester Reader,* ed. Donald McQuade and Robert Atwan, 420. Boston: Bedford Books of St. Martin's Press, 1991.

Tan, Amy. *The Kitchen God's Wife,* 58, 61. New York: Ivy Books, 1991.

Twain, Mark. "Old Times on the Mississippi." In *The Literature of the United States,* 3d ed., ed. Walter Blair, Theodore Hornberger, Randall Stewart, and James E. Miller, Jr., 408–9. Glenview, IL: Scott, Foresman and Company, 1953.

———. *Pudd'nhead Wilson.* In *The Portable Mark Twain,* 557. New York: Viking Press, 1946.

Tyler, Ann. *Dinner at the Homesick Restaurant,* 117. New York: Ivy Books, 1982.

Walker, Alice. Excerpt from *In Search of Our Mothers' Gardens: Womanist Prose.* San Diego: Harcourt Brace Jovanovich, 1983. In *The Norton Reader: An Anthology of Expository Prose,* 9th ed., ed. Linda H. Peterson, Joan E. Hartman, and John C. Brereton, 48. New York: W. W. Norton and Company, 1996.

Wharton, Edith. "The Mission of Jane." In *The Muse's Tragedy and Other Stories,* ed. Candace Wade, 144. London: Penguin Books, 1990.

Wilder, Thornton. *Our Town,* 5–6. 1938. Reprint, New York: Perennial Library, 1985.

Williams, William Carlos. "The Red Wheelbarrow." In *The Literature of the United States,* 3d ed., ed. Walter Blair, Theodore Hornberger, Randall Stewart, and James E. Miller, Jr., 991. Glenview, IL: Scott, Foresman and Company, 1966.

Wright, Richard. *Native Son,* 44–47. New York: Harper and Row Publishers, 1966.

Yeats, William Butler. "The Wild Swans at Coole." In *The Norton Anthology of Poetry,* ed. Arthur M. Eastman, Alexander W. Allison, Herbert Barrows, Caesar R. Blake, Arthur J. Carr, and Hubert M. English, Jr., 912. New York: W. W. Norton and Company, 1970. First published in *The Collected Poems.* New York: Macmillan, 1903.